D0977033

Talking
the Walk

†ALKÏПG †HE WALK

LETTING CHRISTIAN LANGUAGE
Live AGAIN

MARVA DAWП

BrazosPress
Grand Rapids, Michigan

© 2005 by Marva J. Dawn

Published by Brazos Press
a division of Baker Publishing Group
P.O. Box 6287, Grand Rapids, MI 49516-6287
www.brazospress.com

Printed in the United States of America

Library of Congress Cataloging-in-Publication Data
Dawn, Marva J.
    Talking the walk: letting Christian language live again / Marva J. Dawn.
        p.   cm.
    Includes bibliographical references.
    ISBN 1-58743-061-4 (hardcover)
    1. Language and languages—Religious aspects—Christianity.
I. Title.
BR115.L25D39 2005
230′.01′4—dc22   2005001768

CONTENTS

Part III:
Actions of God

GOD

Who do I think I am to begin a book of "corrupted words reclaimed" with *God*? As for who I think I am: a sinner, not capable of this task. Due to God's grace, a servant wanting to point to God. But why claim to reclaim the corrupted word, *God*?

I can't. The name is far too corrupted, trivialized, abstracted, taken in vain, idolized, invoked for the wrong causes.

I begin this book with *God* only because that is all the book is about. It is all that life is about.

Except that we keep forgetting.

At least I know I do.

How easily our lives get filled with all sorts of gods instead of God! And even when we are trying to be faithful, we wind up dishonoring God's name.

I corrupt God's name most by trying to be *its* servant, instead of God's.

I corrupt it some more by marveling at the stupendous works of God's creativity and then forgetting constantly the hidden splendor in the mundane of the ordinary—which isn't so ordinary!

And, of course, I corrupt it further by exploring the profusion of God's attributes and thinking I know God. And perhaps what's worst is that when I've reduced God to my own puny understanding, then I don't trust that diminished God and complain about the sufferings that come my way unfairly (according to me). Good grief! I need God to question me instead of providing cozy little answers to fit my feeble-minded expectations.

7

I corrupt the Holy One's name again when I try to use my best words to begin even to hint at God's cosmic enormity, probing perspicacity, wondrous sublimity, steadfast perpetuity, astute sagacity, intense pity, graceful authority (in my inadequate attempts to imagine and express God's fullness of being). But these are feeble words, and they can only mark the most impotent of beginnings—and not even that unless I know the truth of their frailty.

I corrupt God's name still more by forgetting that every person I encounter bears God's image, that how I treat the passers-by and wheelchair pushers and janitors and military guards in this airport today will reflect that corruption if I don't pay attention.

Ah, yes, the list of my corruptions is endless—so I sit in this quiet corner of an empty airport gate and plead: God beyond my knowing, nothing can be uncorrupted without Your grace. Only by Your mercy can anything be reclaimed. Only in knowing that You are everything and we are nothing without You can we see some Truth.

A toddler and her father have come near me here. She is an exemplary picture for restoring God's name: full-throated exuberance, confident trust in her father, giggling delight in the thrill of walking, intense interest in everything and everyone. Could we learn to live so?

So why do I bother writing another book about God?

Because God is HERE
> and GOD IS.
>> ALL that matters.

That is why everything in this book is about God, even when it might not seem so.

And yes, I know: All of this is so obvious. Why does it need to be said again?

Because I need to hear it.

And so, perhaps, do you.

INTRODUCTION

This book is not intended to be a systematic description of doctrine or an exposition of what we can confidently conclude about the Bible. I'm not qualified for that—and plenty of other people are.

Nor is this book a creative formulation of new approaches to scriptural or doctrinal or church-related issues. I'm not inventive enough—and too many other people try to be.[1]

This book arose as does all my work: when something keeps striking me as a problem in the interrelationships of Christians, churches, and the society around us, I finally feel compelled to do something about it. (As if I could, though at least it's worth a try!)

This book is my response to a crisis in the churches—the frequent corruption or rejection of key words in biblical faith for reasons that often seem to be merely "quick fixes" of, instead of genuine solutions to, deeper problems. Some words like *Father, Lord,* or *Creed* have gotten a bad reputation these days. Some words, like *Hell,* are corrupted by being ignored; some, like *Awesome,* by being overused; some, like *Heaven,* by being dismissed as irrelevant to (post)modern times. As many of these words are replaced—for example, in hymnals—the language changes are often "silly, pernicious, banal, unnecessary, intrusive, and in some cases a perversion of traditional Christian doctrine."[2]

My goal is simply to ask what might be good about the original words, perhaps "to rectify the names."

That phrase comes from Confucius. A collection of his teachings (the Analects) tells of a time when his dim-witted disciple, Tzu-lu, came to him and asked "for the umpteenth

9

time for a simple explanation of all the master's teachings." Tzu-lu asked, specifically, what Confucius would do if the Duke of Wei (who had seized the throne by force) requested the master instead to govern the country. How would he begin? The Master replied that his first step would be to "rectify the names."[3]

Using an example from the U.S. House of Representatives, journalist T. R. Reid explains how such exposure can help us—if we are attentive—to face the truth. He tells of watching the House debate a bill entitled "The Tax Reform and Relief Act of 1980." Typically, this "tax reform" legislation was actually "a collection of special-interest provisions designed to dole out tax breaks to assorted lobby groups." An embattled, bipartisan minority tried to oppose each amendment, but the interest groups had too much power, so "one by one the new tax breaks breezed through to easy passage." Finally, one congressman offered his own amendment to strike the words *Tax Reform* from the title of the bill, since the legislation did not "reform" the tax code at all, but made it more complicated and unfair.

> This quixotic proposal prompted fairly vigorous debate on the floor. The members pushing the tax bill were outraged. What a frivolous amendment! How could the gentleman from Pennsylvania waste the valuable time of this House worrying about the title of the legislation? What difference could it make what the bill was called? .. [but the Congressman responded,] in essence, "A great man named Confucius taught that government cannot operate honestly if the names are dishonest. This amendment to the title of the bill is an attempt at a fundamental goal of good government: the rectification of the names." Naturally, this effort at truth in legislation went down to overwhelming defeat. And Congress is still regularly passing bills called "The Tax Reform Act."[4]

Even as government cannot operate uprightly if the names are dishonest, so churches (and individual Christians) cannot flourish if the names are corrupted. As I travel throughout North America and occasionally to other countries in order to serve the Church (across the denominational spectrum), I am increasingly dismayed that biblical faith is being replaced by something less than faithfulness because of distortions in language. Therefore, this book is a plea, a wee attempt to rectify the names.

During the last century, English-speaking C hristians have been stressing that we should "walk our talk," that our way of living should match the values we espouse. That Christians frequently don't act on what they know and say is still a problem, for the passivity of wealthy societies keeps escalating. However, the opposite is often increasingly true: that the way we talk doesn't offer the deepest truths of the Christian faith. Could we also practice letting the Christian language *live* again in all its glory? Can we work together with the whole Church throughout time and space on rectifying the names and thereby learn more fully to talk our walk?

I won't be able in this one book to restore these words fully, to define or expound them thoroughly. (The endnotes will introduce you to scholars skilled in the necessary biblical, historical, and technical work.) In the true sense of the word *amateur*, I want with love only to reclaim some words significant in the heritage of the Christian faith and to insist that they be properly preserved and embraced for the sake of rectification of the names. They mark key elements in our relationship with God and are vital/lively in faith.

Let me stress that liveliness for a moment. I have seen liturgies or biblical translations or theological books in which the name *God* is repeated over and over again and again *ad nauseum reitero* (to make the point of dull redundancy) in order to avoid using pronouns for the Trinity. But "God . . . God . . . God . . . God . . . God . . ." is not lively.

Pronouns are not necessarily lively words, but they certainly enable literary flow to be more lively. They should be used sparingly and theologically (see below), but why eliminate them entirely (as some publishers and people demand) *a priori*? Let's instead ask this question: Why would we want to reduce the faith by eliminating words before we examine them?

Let me encourage you not to reject any words in this book either until you've pondered them. For example, this book

11

will comment on such things as pronouns for God, but feel free (refraining from judgment) to investigate that at your leisure.

Having been an English literature major through my first masters degree and first years as a teacher (before my life turned more toward theology), I have always been concerned for the power of words, their weightiness, and—when they are abused—their "humiliation."[5] What a delight it was to me, then, to learn that the Hebrew word for "word," *dabar*, eventually began also to signify "event." Do we realize, as well as do the Jews, that our words become events, that how we speak influences what we become and how we behave?

Consequently, I am solemnly concerned about the corruption of words in contemporary Christian faith. When we speak bad theology, we live badly theologically. When our theologians and pastors and communities reject or abuse significant words in the heritage of faith, our Christianity is reduced or decimated. For example, in detailing Robert Funk's (and the Jesus Seminar's) dismissal of the resurrection as a historical reality, Richard Hays notes how surprising it is that Funk "understands himself to be advocating a 'reformation' rather than a refutation of Christianity." After all,

> The resurrectionless story that Funk envisions differs drastically from the story told by the Bible, and the canonical Scriptures of the Old and New Testaments become for him an obstacle to be overcome ("we must find a new plot") rather than a source of good news and life.[6]

When we use other words not from the tradition to deny the meanings of that legacy, is it still Christian faith?

Furthermore, when we corrupt words or use corrupted ones, do we lose our ability to verbalize the faith well? Former University of Chicago professor Joseph Sittler prefigures my concern in this book with this excerpt from *Gravity and Grace*:

> I don't know when it was that I first had my attention called to the combination of precision and magic that words contain. As I reflect back, I still remember how, as a child of about seven

or eight, when I couldn't really understand all of the exalted language, I nevertheless listened week after week to my father as, in a beautiful voice, he read the order of worship. And I remember how certain phrases stuck in my mind. I didn't know exactly what father meant when, reading the liturgy at the Communion, he said, "And therefore with angels and archangels and all the company of heaven," but I knew it was something very big.

And I've never forgotten the beautiful prayer that was appointed for All Saint's Day in the common service book before we reduced our language to absolute flatfootedness. "O Almighty God, Who has knit together Thine elect in one communion and fellowship in the mystical Body of Thy Son. . . ." Somehow today, apparently, we think that's too fancy; but the figure is magnificent. Paul talks about the body of Christ. But the prayer, in a perfectly gorgeous image, talks about the body of Christ and each one of us in it. If you've watched someone knit, you've seen how each stitch is interlocked with every other stitch in such an integral way that if one stitch is dropped, the whole line ravels apart. That's exactly what Paul meant when he said that if one of us suffers, the whole body suffers. But how beautifully the prayer catches it up: "Who hast knit together thine elect . . . in the mystical body of thy Son."

The most accelerated way into understanding what Scripture or any other piece of great literature means is by a fastidious attention to the language. Such fastidiousness is hard to come by these days. We are so benumbed and slugged and diverted, day and night, by radio and television, and in the process we hear language so demeaned and so exaggeratedly used, that the very ability to use words with clarity, precision, and lucidity has become a rare practice in our time.[7]

Because the language is so demeaned and abilities are lost, this project of trying to reclaim corrupted words is much larger than myself, my skills, my training. I wish only to spur us all to some fresh thinking so that perhaps you can carry on from here.

I should admit my presuppositions—but, again, so that you can wrestle with them and see if they are your own, too. I propose that we hold the following statements as "true":

1. The traditional (in the best sense of that word), ortho-dox, catholic faith is intellectually credible.
2. The faith always needs to be rethought in each age and modified in some particulars, but not in essence.
3. The faith always needs to be reclaimed by each genera-tion and not accepted without wrestling.
4. The work of theology is not the province of isolated specialists in the field, but is the struggle, in community, of the whole Church, especially its lay people, whose faith is sometimes threatened and devalued by some professionals.
5. The basic tradition of Christian faith passed on by our forebears is a source of truly meaningful life, of genu-inely loving mission, of infinitely deep delight.

The currents of Christian faith have never been a single stream. The heritage has flowed since its beginning through many channels of interpretation and practice.[8] Yet there are some basic elements of that multifaceted legacy that surge through the common faith of Christians throughout time and space. Some of these are in danger of being dammed by the debris of present theological jargon.

That is a serious problem, but the situation is not hope-less. Nothing that is connected with the Word of God is ever hopeless!

So let this little book offer the claim that some essential words should be retained in all their customary truth and eternal mystery. May it be, in its own tiny way, a prod to all of us to keep thinking deeply about words. Most of all, I pray that this book will glorify God and not dishonor the Triune One. May it enhearten us all a bit and stir us towards deeper love for God and our neighbors.

PART 1

GOD

JESUS

"Jeeeeee-sus Christ!" the collegian behind me growled, as I plodded with a load of Bibles in my backpack up the monstrously long flight of stairs to the student union building for a university Bible study. I turned to him and said, "I wish you wouldn't use that tone of voice when you name the person I love the most."

If looks could kill, I'd be dead—but I was tired of hearing the corruption of Jesus' name by mindless cursing. Naively I thought I could at least make it a little less mindless or perhaps even end the cursing. Little did I expect, young as I was, how numerous would be the ways that Jesus' name is corrupted in church life and theology.

I'm not claiming innocence. I know I corrupt His name, too, and will do so until that glorious day when I know Him face to face. There are times now, I admit, when I really wonder who He was, what He truly said, why He did what He did, and what He means now and in the future for my life and the world. He is infinitely beyond our human capacities for understanding, of course, but at least if we were more careful we could avoid some of the more common pitfalls of defamation.

Why does Jesus cause such problems? Even such prestigious journals as the *New York Times* have used the phrase *Jesus Wars* to report some of the controversies surrounding His life and mission.

Undoubtedly, the most significant difficulties have arisen because of the conflict between what Luke Timothy Johnson calls "the Misguided Quest for the Historical Jesus" and "the Truth of the Traditional Gospels."[1] How much can we know

17

about the actual life of Jesus of Nazareth? How much can we trust the accounts of the Gospel writers? How much can we depend on what the Church has passed on about Him?[2]

That He existed we do not doubt. There is too much historical documentation by those who didn't believe in Him to dispute His actuality. But what do we make of Him?

A few impressions become more deeply embedded in me the more I ponder the Gospel narratives. Notably, the life of Jesus that they report is too delightful, too astounding, too real, too exceptionally contrary to everyone's expectations (including the Gospel writers') to be fabricated. Jesus is also too much the contrary of expectations to be easily dismissed. He fascinates me, draws me, woos me with His compassion. And there is too much internal coherence in the descriptions of His life, miracles, teachings, sufferings, death, resurrection, and ascension to deny one part without disqualifying the whole. I finally have to accept what is said about Him or else find another way to account for the magnetism of the man, the power of His message, the integrity of the witness concerning Him.

I can't get Him out of my mind. It seems that what He teaches is the only cogent and compelling way to live in the world. But He demands too much of me—and perhaps that is the major reason that most distrust the historicity of the biblical narratives. Perhaps some scholars want to deny the truth of the Gospel accounts of Jesus because they don't want to obey what the Scriptures say He said and did. God's way of working in Jesus is indeed a hidden way, a way of weakness and humility, suffering and death.

What surprises me most is that those who deny Jesus' miracles or the Gospel records of His teaching can't really justify His crucifixion. Some scholars who insist that we can't trust the biblical accounts for anything resembling history insist that Jesus simply died as the result of human hate. But why would religious leaders hate Him so—unless there were such things as the (implicit) Messianic claims that the Gospels recount? His death, in the form it took, could not have been the "natural" result of His life if that life matched the reductions such theologians make of His work and teachings to eliminate their God-claims.

On the other side, those who insist on Jesus' divinity often don't want the sheer immensity and thoroughness of His suffering either. They want a triumphant God, a Victor who enables them to be victors, too, in daily life. But we are talking about Jesus, the Suffering Servant, who showed us that God's way to work is through affliction and even humiliation for the sake of others. Are we not willing to live and die the Lamb's way?

If we want to reclaim the name *Jesus* with all the fullness of His character, can we ignore His call, "Follow me," and His rebuke, "Unless you take up your cross and follow Me, you cannot be My disciples"? (He didn't say, "Take up your teddy bear and follow Me"!) It seems His name is corrupted because we really don't want to share His death. We don't want to believe that to give ourselves over into death for the sake of life is still the way that God in Jesus works in the world—and the only way to live, despite the circumstances, with infinite gladness!

HE, HIS, HIM, HIMSELF

Perhaps you are bothered by my use of these pesky "masculine" pronouns. They have been corrupted, of course, by patriarchal Christians who use them to leave out the female half of the world, to limit opportunities for women, to invent a masculine God, to justify all sorts of oppressions.

On the other hand, the words are corrupted when, in the midst of a worship service, the liturgy employs a masculine pronoun and a person next to us shouts out "God" or "she" instead and disrupts our concentration and adoration. Protests do not belong in services of worship devoted to *public* praise of God.

I confess that at first I didn't understand feminist objections to masculine pronouns for God. Though I had grown up in a quite patriarchal family and very patriarchal denomination and had, because of patriarchal politics, been denied two faculty positions for which I was chosen, still I was comfortable with the words *He, His, Him*, and *Himself*. Because they were capitalized when I was a child, they didn't signify God's "maleness" to me at all. Instead they carried a sense of the ineffable, the holy—and yet, being personal words, they conveyed the secret but revealed wonder of the lofty God's immanence (or closeness to me). They were cozy words, I thought.

Gradually I came to appreciate the truth of objections to pronouns for God because church history is filled with patriarchal tyrannies. I have experienced more than enough of that myself, even in graduate schools and certainly in churches. Besides, apart from the embodied Jesus, God is obviously neither masculine nor feminine, but more than all our inadequate language could ever convey.

Increasingly, however, I have come to think that the real problem with pronouns for God is that we stopped capitalizing them. Lowercase pronouns for God are too human; they look more obviously gender biased. When the pronouns are not capitalized, the words can no longer convey this mystery: that the transcendent God is also personal, that the Wholly Other is Holy and still *for us*!

Too bad English is not like Hungarian, in which pronouns for the third person singular signify both masculine and feminine. Could we use the Hungarian *"ö"* for "he/she," *"öt"* for "him/her," and *"övé"* for "his/hers"?[3] Or perhaps we could join the Chinese, who use one character for "he/she/it" and attach it to the separate sign that means "God" in order to create a pronoun that is distinctly God's pronoun.

Instead, some religious leaders use specifically feminine pronouns for God. The problem with that option is that *she, hers, her,* and *herself* were not considered inclusive in the English language until recently. Consequently, whenever we read or listen and suddenly encounter one of these pronouns, English speakers automatically think in gender terms and find God thereby reduced to the feminine or to an argument.

What we need instead is more creativity as we use the vast treasures of biblical names for God. Names like *the Holy One, the* LORD, or *the Almighty* are more desirable because they expand our thoughts about God instead of diminish them.

However, sometimes there simply are problems with literary flow. Pronouns were invented to help languages move more easily. To say, "Myron just brought me flowers from my husband's garden; Mr. Sandberg is such a kind person, but doesn't envision Myron's-self that way—I need to tell Myron that more" is downright ludicrous compared to "Myron just brought me flowers from his garden; he is such a kind person, but doesn't envision himself that way—I need to tell him more." Why make our language unnecessarily cumbersome when we have the gift of pronouns?

Though our language is always inadequate anyway, one partial alleviation of the pronoun problem is to be more trinitarian. We can name particular persons of the Trinity more specifically and, when speaking of Jesus, use masculine pronouns—since, indeed, He was truly male.

Some reject Jesus' maleness on the grounds that it is oppressive to women to think about God in gendered terms, but God *had to be* incarnated as a man in order to model and teach true servanthood. Women may resent the servant role, for they are too often forced into that situation and reduced to servility. But when Jesus, a strong male carpenter and honored rabbi, demonstrates tenderness and compassion, we see the odd, countercultural servanthood of God's infinite mercy[4] and learn what John Yoder calls "revolutionary subordination."[5]

Though now I try to avoid pronouns for the other persons of the Trinity (when it is possible without violating speakable English), they are appropriate for Jesus. I capitalize them to emphasize that He was/is no ordinary man. Male pronouns for God that appear in biblical texts cited in this book are capitalized; could they remind us that we know God precisely and thoroughly through the triune incarnation in the man Jesus? Could we reclaim the biblical truth that such pronouns signify not gender, but the astonishing mystery of the cosmic Trinity's relational intimacy with us through Jesus and His enfleshment for our sake?

Messiah (or the Christ)

In His conversation with the Samaritan woman in John 4:25–26, Jesus applies the title of Messiah (Hebrew) or Christ (Greek) to Himself. The issue pervades all of the Gospels: is this Jesus of Nazareth the fulfillment of First Testament prophecies, the bearer of the divine work for the sake of God's people, the deliverer from oppression and shame and sin?

The contemporary fashion to corrupt the name *Messiah* by separating the man Jesus from the Christ of the Church is actually not a new disorder. Heretics in the first centuries of the Church separated Jesus from Christ by saying that only the man Jesus suffered, while Christ the divine One remained impassible.[6]

When I simply *listen* to all the references in the four Gospels to the Greek *christos* (translated "Messiah" in NRSV), I can't help but be struck by so many usages that are confident testimonies to the belief that this Jesus was the Messiah. Matthew, the narrator, proclaims it assuredly four times in his first chapter. In Mark, Peter is the first to use the title (8:29; cf. Matt. 16:16, 20 and Luke 9:20), though Jesus also answers affirmatively that He is the Messiah when questioned in 14:62. In Luke, the angels and Simeon know Jesus is the Messiah when He is still a baby (ch. 2), and the demons affirm it in chapter 4. Andrew, Martha, and the Gospel's writer all declare it in John (1:41, 11:27, 20:31).

In contrast, the Gospels also contain several debates about the title (e.g., John 7), misunderstandings about the designation even among Jesus' own disciples and forerunner (Matt. 11:2), expulsion from the synagogue for those who believe Jesus is the Messiah (John 9:22), and plenty of ambiguity in

Jesus' answers when He is asked whether or not He is the Messiah (Matt. 26:63; Luke 22:67; John 10:24–38). These confusions surely contribute to many of today's problems with the name *Christ*.

Do those who insist that Jesus of Nazareth is not the same as the Christ of faith want that division in order not to make too much of Jesus? Then what, besides seeing Messianic hopes and convictions fulfilled, would have given rise to the early use of the title and, even more suggestive, the rejection of Jesus by the religious leaders of His time? Did Peter make his emphatic assertion, or was that put into his mouth by later writers? The contexts of his declaration in the various Gospels seems always to suggest that the problem was not that he made the statement, but that he didn't know what it meant.

On the opposite side of the theological spectrum, some who accept the Gospel accounts of various uses of the title of "the Christ" don't really live as though that name designates Messianic work undertaken by suffering and a cross. They insist on a successful Christ who enables them to live comfortably, in wealth and luxury, without enemies or troubles or sacrifice.

Jesus' words to Cleopas and his companion should still burden us, "Was it not necessary that the Messiah should suffer these things and then enter into his glory?" (Luke 24:26). Those who overemphasize the victorious Christ move too quickly to His glory; those who divide between Jesus of Nazareth and the Christ of faith move too slowly to His glory and want to deny the hints of it in Jesus' earthly life and work. Perhaps underneath it all both sides of the theological spectrum are struggling with the same thing: to accept Jesus as the Christ throughout His life necessarily means that *God* always intended to work through weakness and death, and that implies that the Trinity still works in such a way.[7]

If "repentance and the forgiveness of sins [are] to be proclaimed *in His name* to all nations" (Luke 24:47, emphasis mine), then Christ's name—which also implies His character—must be truly ours, too. Do we bear the name *Christian* in weakness and death?

LORD

Many today discard or avoid the name *Lord* for Jesus or the Triune God. The word has been corrupted, of course, especially by unjust and cruel medieval lords who exploited their peasants—their tyrannies multiplied by the many tales about them—but does that necessitate renouncing the word entirely?

Some people appear to reject the word because they don't like the idea that God has the right to demand obedience from us; they forget that Christ's is a generous and considerate lordship, overflowing with such abundant love that we *want* to obey. A word that is a source of relief and hope to me makes such people recoil rather than rejoice.

We lose substantially important gifts for faith if we capriciously dismiss God's title, *Lord*. However, the term does have its peculiar ambiguities, so we can't reclaim it easily.

Perhaps we could winnow out some problems if we first separated the two very different Hebrew words that can be rendered by the English "lord." One term, *adonai*, meaning some sort of "superior," is used in the First Testament for all sorts of lords—one's master, governor, prince, leader. The biblical title does sometimes designate oppressive people, but it certainly never indicates that when it is capitalized and used to speak of God.

The other Hebrew word, rendered "Lord" (with ORD in a smaller capitalization), is more precisely a name—the four consonants, *YHWH*, which we don't know how to pronounce since written Hebrew originally included no vowel points. Faithful Jewish believers would not say this name aloud (or even in their minds) in order to avoid blaspheming it. In the past, English speakers verbalized it as "Jehovah," but now it is usually expressed as "Yahweh."

I love this word, for it signifies the "I AM," the name God revealed to Moses at the burning bush. The French wisely use "L'Eternel" for *YHWH* (and "le Seigneur" for *adonai*). It is a name which reminds us always of God's covenant promises, God's character of fidelity in spite of our disloyalty. It is a name that comforts and sustains me, for if God IS and always WAS and WILL BE, then I can trust in God no matter what my circumstances might be.

YHWH is never a term for tyranny. It is always a title of infinite compassion and mercy, of constant faithfulness and steadfast love. Particularly, it is one of the main words that links the Covenant God of the First Testament with Jesus in the New through His use of the phrase "I am."[8]

In the New Testament the Greek word for "lord," *kyrios*, carries the meanings of both *YHWH* and *adonai*. Sometimes *kyrios* is used for God; sometimes, for Jesus particularly; and elsewhere, for subjects of parables, Roman leaders, or simply as a term of respect.

We can't help but wonder, How did the biblical writers intend the word when they applied it to Jesus? Did the original speakers mean "Lord" in the sense of *adonai* or of *YHWH*? When did they first start using the title for Jesus in the latter sense? In other words, at what point did His followers start recognizing Him as God?

When the apostle Paul writes, "if you confess with your lips that Jesus is Lord and believe in your heart that God raised Him from the dead, you will be saved" (Rom. 10:9), we might think at first that he's using "Lord" in the sense of *adonai*. But a few verses later, he makes Jesus' divinity clear when he applies Joel 2:32 to Jesus—"Everyone who calls on the name of the LORD shall be saved."

Paul also emphasizes that Jesus Christ's Lordship links God's people together. In 1 Corinthians 1:2 he writes "To the church of God that is in Corinth, to those who are sanctified in Christ Jesus, called to be saints, together with all those who in every place call on the name of our Lord Jesus Christ, both their Lord and ours." Do those who reject this wonderful name *Lord* not want to be united with all other Christians? What do they have against us?

Both Paul and the book of Acts tell us that Jesus has been made our Lord. The great hymn of Christ's humiliation in Philippians 2:5–11 culminates with this great acclamation: "Therefore God also highly exalted Him and gave Him the name that is above every name, so that at the name of Jesus every knee should bend, in heaven and on earth and under the earth, and every tongue should confess that Jesus Christ is Lord, to the glory of God the Father."

Similarly, Luke records Peter's Pentecost sermon with this pithy conclusion: "Therefore let the entire house of Israel know with certainty that God has made Him both Lord and Messiah, this Jesus whom you crucified" (Acts 2:36). What a privilege to call Jesus "Lord"!

Why would we ever want to lose all the gifts of this name *Lord*? It identifies Jesus as the biblical God of covenant faithfulness; by it we bear witness to His divinity and His headship over a unified Church.

Jesus has never been oppressive in His Lordship over me, though I have often rejected His authority or rebelled against it—so by confessing that He is my Lord I am submitting gladly to Him for the transformation of my life. Do those who reject His name *Lord* not want this privilege and this responsibility and this challenge: "As you therefore have received Christ Jesus the Lord, continue to live your lives in Him, rooted and built up in Him and established in the faith, just as you were taught, abounding in thanksgiving" (Col. 2:6)?

OUR LORD JESUS CHRIST

This full name, or any combination of two or three of its words, is mishandled in all sorts of ways—by rejecting the idea of Jesus' lordship, by dividing Jesus of Nazareth from the Christ of faith or contrarily treating the word *Christ* as the last name of Jesus, by trivializing the full meaning of the phrase, by calling on the person the name designates but refusing truly to bow to Him. I know I'm especially guilty of the latter. Recently I severely burned my crippled foot, and I'm still rebelling by throwing myself a pity party and bemoaning that any good lord worth his salt would not let such things happen in his world. (Yes, I didn't capitalize those last two pronouns because when I rage I forget who He is.)

Even after reflecting on its separate parts, I'm including this segment on "Our Lord Jesus Christ" because throughout the New Testament we can't help but notice how the early Church loved this full name. Combinations of "Jesus," "Christ," and "Lord" occur 52 times in the New Testament in at least four different sequences—and in the entire range of the books, from four times in the earliest, 1 Thessalonians, to seven times in the much later books, 2 Peter and Jude.

Throughout the Gospels we can see progressions in thought and almost hear the disciples wrestling with whether this Jesus could be the Christ—and, if so, what that might mean. For example, as Rikk Watts taught at a recent Regent College pastors' conference, consider Jesus stilling the storm and then sending Legion into the pigs, who then plunged into the sea (Mark 4:37–5:13). Observe the disciples' terror. Remember that they were good Jews, so they knew from Exodus 14 Who alone could tell the sea what to do and then threw His enemies into it! Consequently, while they followed Jesus and lived together, they became increasingly aware that someone extraordinary was with them and probably gradually became convinced of the truth that Jesus is God's Christ, even if, before the gift of the Holy Spirit, they weren't really prepared to face the consequences for their own lives or His. In the end, they couldn't help but call Him their Lord.

The same is true for us—the more we live with Jesus, especially as we work through defeat and death to the Resurrection, we can't help but agree with the essential conviction that the Messiah was more than an agent sent by God; Christ is the LORD Himself.

As William Placher observes, the story of Jesus always knits two *what*s into one *who*. That is, "if we ask *what* Jesus Christ was, there are two answers: he was God, and he was a human being."[9] His words and deeds—to forgive sins, to raise the dead, to accomplish our redemption—could only be said and done by God. He also lived in very human ways—eating meals, sleeping. But always it was only one person, Jesus Christ, who did them.[10]

The Bible never defines how this inconceivable unity is achieved; rather, the Scriptures *display* it for us through narratives. "Christ cures a blind man—but he does it by applying his own spit. He thus does a divine thing in a very human way. He died on a cross, but he does it in a way that wins our salvation, thus doing the most human of things in a divine way."[11]

No one can explain it. As the apostle Paul exclaims in reference to another perplexity, "O the depth of the riches and wisdom and knowledge of God! . . . how inscrutable His ways!" (Rom. 11:33). Can we do anything but stand back in utter astonishment and celebrate the God of such impossible mysteries and submit to Him as Lord?

The Council of Chalcedon in 451 resorted to negatives. Since we cannot explain the person of Jesus the Christ, we can only adore Him and acknowledge what errors we must avoid in thinking about our Lord:

29

In agreement, therefore, with the holy fathers, we all unanimously teach that we should confess that our Lord Jesus Christ is one and the same Son, the same perfect in Godhead and the same perfect in manhood, truly God and truly man . . . one and the same Christ, Son, Lord, only-begotten, made known in two natures without confusion, without change, without division, without separation . . . the Lord Jesus Christ . . .[12]

Earlier, Gregory of Nazianzus had expressed his wonder and gratitude at the Lordship of Jesus the Christ in this way:

He hungered—but he fed thousands. . . . He was wearied, but he is the rest of them that are weary and heavy-laden. . . . He prays but He hears prayer. . . . He is sold, and very cheap, for it is only for thirty pieces of silver; but he redeems the world and that at a great price, for the price was his own blood. . . . As a sheep he is led to the slaughter, but he is the shepherd of Israel, and now of the whole world, also. As a lamb he is silent, yet he is the Word, and is proclaimed by the voice of one crying in the wilderness. He is bruised and wounded, but he heals every disease and every infirmity. . . . He dies, but gives life, and by his death destroys death.[13]

Maybe our modernist need to control everything by scientific explanation and our postmodern need to deconstruct dogma need to be exchanged for a more awed beholding, a more humble bowing before, and a more ardent and radiant knitting of our lives to, the God-Man Jesus the Christ, our Lord.

Behold!

I love the word *Behold*! It is a "grab you by the shirt collar and shake you up a little" word. When it appears in the King James Version and other older translations, it renders an exclamatory word from the original Hebrew or Greek that often is followed by the text revealing something astonishing about God.

Sadly, in some cases now the new translations completely leave out the exclamation or wimp it down into a pathetic verb like "See" or something equally innocuous. In our visually overloaded, hasty culture we regularly see all sorts of things that we never bother to notice. Often when we are seeing or even looking, we are not paying the remotest attention.

Why on earth would I include here in this book's section discussing names for God a lament for the corruption by omission of the word *Behold*? My stimulus was reading about an ancient Eastern Orthodox icon of the Transfiguration in which the disciples appear all askew, as if they have been hurled further down the mountain. Archbishop of Canterbury Rowan Williams explains that they have been caught in the tidal wave of God's life eternally flowing through the Son, the Word.[14] Similarly, all the names for God we ever encounter should stop us short, unsettle us, and remind us that they surely convey infinitely more than we could ever imagine or hope.

Couldn't we find more dramatic invitations than "See" if we have to replace "Behold!"—like the British "Mind your head!", the military "Listen up!", or the chant of Orthodox priests before reading a lesson from the Scriptures, "Attend!"?

The problem is that most of our consciousness-raising calls are not elegant, lofty, or startling enough. They don't quite have the zing; they don't quite make us realize that we've just been thrown down the Mount of Transfiguration.

But, people complain, "Behold!" is not a word customarily used in our society. That's precisely why it's so good.

KING

Some object to calling Jesus or the Triune God "King" on the grounds that the word is decisively (and therefore oppressively) masculine. Besides, some say, we no longer have kings and so the image doesn't communicate. The biblical name has been dishonored by being spurned.

Yet children still hear fairy tales of kings and queens. We still talk of sports heroes as the king of basketball or the queen of tennis. We still use expressions like "kingpin," and children still play "king on the mountain."

We need the image of Christ/God the King to remember how upside down the world is in its visions of leadership. And the masculine gender is not a problem if we remember why the Kingship of Jesus, the perfect fulfillment of all that the name *King* could connote, is so astonishing in its humility and empowerment for others.

The world's kings have been known for their brutalities and aggressions, their military victories, their global powers, their despoiling of women, their unjust taxations, their enslavement of enemies. Jesus comes to set things right, to show (contrary to all expectations of maleness) a servant's heart and life. He honors women and gives them their true mission. He offers His gifts gratuitously and sets prisoners free. His power is that of vulnerability; His victory arises from His willing defeat. His is a reign of justice and righteousness, a kingdom that will stand against all the powers of evil.

How can we respond in any way but to "rejoice greatly" and to "shout aloud"? Behold! our one true King comes to us "triumphant and victorious . . . , humble and riding on a donkey," a symbol of peace. He cuts off the chariots and the war horses and the battle bows and instead "shall command peace to the nations. . . . His dominion [stretches] from sea to sea . . . because of the blood of [His] covenant with [us]" (Zech. 9:9–11).

How can we not but greet this King with our red carpets and cloaks, with our acclaim and our selves? How can we not but want Him to reign in all of our lives—especially as we wait for His reign over the entire cosmos to be revealed?

GOOD SHEPHERD

How could the lovely name *Good Shepherd* be corrupted? Perhaps the fact that many of us immediately associate loveliness or coziness with it is perhaps a sign of its distortion.

The name is corrupted if I coddle myself by imagining being carried as a lamb in the arms of a strong shepherd when I should probably be prodded with a stout rod instead. The former comfortable image was fostered by the stained glass window at the front of the sanctuary where I worshiped as a child. It depicted a not-very-Jewish, pristine Jesus surrounded by docile and purely white sheep. That window held no hints of the rough work of shepherding or the earthiness and stupidity of sheep.

The lamb being carried in the window was cute and clean, a creature you certainly would want to rescue. It didn't show me what a lost lamb would really look like—scraggly, mud-caked, maybe bloody, stinky, really LOST.

In reaction to such sentimentality some people want to throw out the biblical name and metaphor entirely. We don't know shepherds any more, some insist; we ought to use a technologically relevant metaphor.

That is precisely the problem. In our scientifically advanced and commodified world we are so removed from the actuality of the land—the source of our food and water, the humus from which our humanity is derived—that we don't recognize an image that demands someone's life. And technology usually calls for tinkering, a quick fix. It doesn't show us how desperately unable we are to rescue ourselves.

Jesus uses the image to show us the extent to which He will go on our behalf. He will enter society with the lowest of the low. He will lay down His life for the sheep. (John 10:11–18 records that more than once.)

My friend John in Australia is a shepherd. He loves his sheep, cares for them passionately. When we visited him for a few days, we saw how carefully he planned where to move them to make sure they had food. We watched him chase a stray ram, wrestle it down and throw it into his truck to move it to its proper place. We witnessed the truth that sheep really do know their master's voice; they would follow John, but would not heed us or any other stranger. Since Australia has experienced a severe drought, John's anxiety for the sheep has been apparent as the dams for drinking water have dried up. His whole life—and that of his family—is devoted to his sheep. It's not a lucrative way to farm these days, but John's love for sheep is evident when he talks about them and tries to get me to sound Aussie when I say, "fine sheep's wool."

At his farm we also observed the idiocy of sheep as they chased around in circles and wedged themselves into an increasingly tight huddle. They absolutely can't get along without John.

Mull over the absurdity if we chase accumulations of entertainments and gadgets, but fail to invest in deep friendships and family bonds. Consider the circles we run—scrambling for time and then cluttering it up with senseless superficiality, jostling for fame and finding it vacuous. Ponder the huddles into which we wedge ourselves—estranged from our neighbors and the world by our selfishness and inhospitality, cultural arrogance and immorality, national militance and flagrant waste.

What idiots are we that we so often act as if we could get along without a good shepherd?

SON OF MAN

Did Jesus know who He was? Did He apply the phrase *Son of Man* to Himself as a title and, if so, why—or did the early Church apply it to Him later? Was Jesus aware that He was totally human and totally divine—or is that a later ascription or even invention?

These are intriguing questions that raise various debates, which can't necessarily be resolved, especially since we can't crawl inside Jesus' mind to determine what He knew about Himself. I bring up the topic because these controversies have led to a problematic corruption in biblical translations—but let's look at that later. Let me set up the mystery first. (Too bad there were no tape recorders in Jesus' day so that we could know the answers with historical certainty!)

The troubles arise because the Hebrew phrase, best rendered *son of adam* (related to *adamah* or earth), normally means "human being" or "humanity" or, as the NRSV renders it, "mortal." Ezekiel contains 93 instances, most likely to contrast the prophet's creatureliness with the infinite sovereignty of the LORD who speaks to and through him.

But Daniel 7:13–18 declares that one "like a son of man" receives from the Ancient of Days divine powers and authority. The ambiguity of the meaning of "Son of Man" is intensified because of what are called the parables of Enoch (1 Enoch 37–71). These employ the phrase decisively as a title and associate "Son of Man" with the preexistence of God's Word, with the Suffering Servant imagery of Isaiah, with Daniel's vision, and with other obviously Messianic language. The problem is that we don't know when Enoch was written—and whether it was written by a Christian. Which is the chicken and which the egg—a tradition of "Son of Man" as a Messianic term or Jesus' use of the phrase, perhaps simply to emphasize His humanity? (The chicken and egg are quite scrambled by those who think Jesus didn't say "Son of Man" about Himself, but insist that the phrase is a later addition by the Church.)

I could live with the ambiguities and simply still appreciate all the implications of the title, were it not for the way in which the NRSV translation of Daniel 7:13 has already prejudiced the case. This translation is corrupted first by the gender politics that renounces the words *Son* and *man*. Correlatively, many times a biblical "sons" is replaced by the word *children*, which doesn't carry the same connotations of responsibility, privilege, and maturity as the idea of sonship.

But another level of corruption is added to Daniel 7:13, which is translated in the NRSV as "I saw one like a *human being* coming with the clouds of heaven. And he came to the Ancient One and was presented before him" (emphasis mine). Since the NRSV retains the designation *Son of Man* in all the New Testament uses of the correlative Greek phrase (*ho hios tou anthropou*), it looks overly political to remove the title from Daniel, which is the origin of the Messianic associations of the "Son of Man." Wouldn't it be preferable, instead, if ordinary believers reading Daniel could be reminded of their greater familiarity with the title as used by and for Jesus in the New Testament and thereby notice in the seer's vision a truly prophetic description of Jesus receiving "dominion and glory and kingship"?

Truly, the Church knows that Christ alone reveals a dominion that "is an everlasting dominion that shall not pass away," and a kingship "that shall never be destroyed" (Dan. 7:14). Should a biblical translation eliminate the possibility (I think likelihood) that Jesus used the phrase for Himself to show that His dominion was not only that of the returning Judge, but also of one in the present who had the right to forgive sins and who secured salvation for us in the extraordinary act of God becoming flesh in order to die as all flesh must?

The plethora of situations in which the Gospel narrators record Jesus naming Himself "Son of Man" (77 times in an extensive diversity of circumstances) increases my conviction that Jesus did apply the phrase to Himself. The likelihood that He employed it with Messianic overtones is bolstered because He employs the title often in connection with statements that reveal an entirely different picture from that of Daniel.

Look, for example, at more than one third of the 30 cases in Matthew. Jesus remarks that the Son of Man has nowhere to lay His head (8:20), is criticized for eating with sinners (11:19), will be in the earth as Jonah was in the whale (12:40), will suffer (17:12) and be betrayed (17:22; 20:18; 26:2, 24, 45) and crucified (17:22–23) as a ransom for many (20:28).

Other texts in Matthew include such diverse comments as that the Son of Man has authority to forgive sins (9:6), is Lord of the Sabbath (12:8), can be spoken against and still be forgiven (in contrast to the Spirit, 12:32), is the sower in His parable (13:37, 41). In only a third of Matthew's instances is the reference specifically to the Son of Man coming in glory; some of those compare His coming to lightning (24:27) or to the days of Noah in its unexpectedness (24:37, 39, 44). Another two occurrences are in connection with the Transfiguration (16:28; 17:9). Luke (as may be expected) includes most of the same instances as Matthew, but Mark cites a higher proportion of cases where Jesus names Himself "Son of Man" contrary to Daniel's vision.

But did Jesus intend the phrase to be a reference to the vision of Daniel 7? How much did He know about Himself and when did He know it?

Perhaps we could be helped by imagining what it must have been like for Jesus growing up. All of us learn from our parents something of who we are. Think about the character of His mother Mary. Why did God choose her for the virginal conception and to raise Jesus? Luke (who, many scholars think, knew Mary personally) demonstrates that she was a devout Jewish young woman. Certainly she would have shared her "ponderings" with her boy as He grew up; indeed, she would have made sure that He had opportunities in the synagogue to become immersed in the teachings of the Hebrew prophets, history, and writings. And would she not have told Him about the unusual circumstances of His conception and birth?[15]

Though His followers had a really tough time catching on, doesn't it make sense to think that Jesus knew who He was?

Why does all this matter to me? Personally I am overwhelmed with gratitude that God should stoop so far as to become truly mortal, actually a human being, to demonstrate to us what God's "everlasting dominion and glory and kingship" as envisioned by Daniel genuinely are and will be. I don't have to be able to explain it; I can only exclaim it: God with us, Son of Man in the flesh, reigns over the cosmos!

SON OF GOD

Since the previous entry, "Son of Man," immersed us in mystery, we might as well raise another issue that pits those who trust the Bible as truthful testimony against those who doubt the veracity of its witness to who Jesus was. Do we rightly ascribe to Jesus the title *Son of God*, though He never uses it for Himself in the Synoptics?

The issue is sharpened in the scene in which Jesus asks His disciples who they say that He is. When Peter responds in Matthew 16:16, "You are the Messiah, the Son of the living *God*," Jesus goes on after that confession to describe the Son of *Man* as one who will be betrayed, tortured, and crucified (Matt. 16:21–26; see also Mark 8:31–37, Luke 9:21–25). In addition, in all three Gospels Jesus concludes with a reference to the Son of Man's coming in glory and the promise that some would see that glory (in the Transfiguration) before tasting death (Matt. 16:27–28, Mark 8:38–9:1, Luke 9:26–27). Does He thereby equate "Son of God" with "Son of Man," while offering an elaboration of the significance of those two titles by means of the tension of their contrast?

Books from the whole spectrum of the New Testament give the testimony that Jesus is "the Son of God." In early writings Paul uses the phrase for Jesus in Romans 1:4; 2 Corinthians 1:19; and Galatians 2:20. (Acts 9:20 suggests that Paul began using the title for Jesus immediately after his conversion.) Later uses include one in Ephesians, four in Hebrews, and seven in 1 John.

The Gospels contain a variety of instances of this designation for Jesus. Each narrator except Matthew names Jesus with the title—Mark to begin his Gospel (1:1), John to end

41

God

his (20:31), and Luke (see below) in his genealogy (3:38). Matthew finds it negatively in the mouth of the devil (4:3, 6; cf. Luke 4:3, 9), a demoniac (8:29), the crowds (27:40), and the high priest (26:63) and positively in the response of the disciples to the rescue of Peter and the stilling of the storm (14:33) and in the centurion's response to events at His death (27:54; see also Mark 15:39). Mark (3:11) and Luke (4:41) hear the unclean spirits shout the title, and Luke adds its use by the crowds and religious leaders (22:70) and the angel Gabriel (1:35).

John records the title most extensively. Only once is the title thrown out in accusation by the crowds (19:7), but John the Baptizer, Nathaniel, and Martha all use it with praise (1:34, 1:49, and 11:27, respectively). Only in writings associated with John does Jesus use the title for Himself (John 3:18, 5:25, 10:36, 11:4 and Rev. 2:18).

Why does all this matter? Why is the title important?

Two contemporary corruptions plague this phrase. Some (besides Jehovah Witnesses) suggest that the use of the title does not equate in meaning with the word *God*, but corresponds instead with the way that all of us are children of God (as Luke uses the title in his genealogy). The other problem arises from those who separate the title from the historical person Jesus of Nazareth as a much later usage by the Church.

In response to the first, I point to the diversity of voices that utter the title in the entire New Testament. The devil is recorded as using the designation in his attempts to dissuade Jesus from God's way of working in the world. Unclean spirits and demoniacs shriek it in alarm, one would think, because they recognize that they are up against the power of God Himself. If Luke actually interviewed Mary as some scholars suggest, then she heard the title from an angel of heaven (and that angel didn't address her in the same way!). Most important, the ones who use the title in praise are responding to acts of God in miracles (see Part III), at conversion, or in fulfillment of inspiration (see John 1:32–34).

The opinion that the title was a much later addition to the Christian faith is made suspect by the fact that the title appears in books from the entire period of New Testament writing, and because the accusation that Jesus named Himself God's Son is hurled at Him at His crucifixion (Matt. 27:43; John 19:7). These Gospels and letters were not written to prove or even develop the idea that Jesus was God; rather, Jesus' followers already believed Him to be God, and that is the reason that these texts were written and preserved in the first place. As John Yoder reminds us,

> We only have the oldest texts *because* of the high Christology. And that same Christology made people, after most of the rest of the New Testament was written, very concerned to hold fast to all they could possibly reclaim about the earthly career of the man they already celebrated as risen Lord.[16]

A high percentage of theologians these days approach biblical texts with what is called a "hermeneutics of suspicion," suggesting that interpretation should be characterized more by skepticism than by easy acceptance. Who do we think God is? Is it not possible that God would *want* us to have truthful testimony to triune involvement with our world and would watch over the process of its recording?

Is it not possible that Jesus' closest friend, the beloved disciple John, would rightly recall becoming convinced of His divinity and would faithfully give testimony to that realization (John 20:31, 21:24)? Just as we today experience the presence of God at work among us by the power of the Holy Spirit, wasn't the faith passed on from the beginning—and died for—because people knew that God had walked among them in the person of God's "beloved Son"?[17]

WORD

Isn't it funny that a religion centered in One who is named "Word" has become so sloppy with its words? I don't mean just with rejections of doctrinal terms, but also with careless or overly sentimentalized song or liturgy writing, with illiteracy concerning the words of the Scriptures which give testimony to the Word, with increasing dependence upon the visual to convey our faith in the Word to the world around us, and with diminished ability to hear God speak in a voice that contradicts our society's words about values and ideologies.

You'd think that if we really believed that Jesus is God's Word, who is both God and with-God for us, we'd spend more time listening to the Word, more attention to living it, and more concern for what we say and how we say it.

FATHER, SON, AND HOLY SPIRIT

These days many people like to replace this list of the three persons in the Trinity with terms like "Creator, Redeemer, Sanctifier." Those who corrupt the trinitarian title this way usually contend that they change the names because such terms as *Father* and *Son* (q.v.) are offensive. They are exclusive, masculine, oppressive to women, outdated.

The problem is that "Creator," "Redeemer," and "Sanctifier" aren't names; they designate functions. In truth, these functions are performed by all three persons in the Godhead, so the words not only don't actually name them, but also the terms don't distinguish them.

For instance, creation is not limited to God the Father. Such texts as John 1:3 and 10; John 3:6; Luke 1:35; 2 Corinthians 3:5–6; Galatians 5:22, and Colossians 1:16–17 suggest that all three persons are involved in creation. The same could be exhibited for any functional words. In fact, some of the patriarchal corruptions of redemption have arisen because people ignored the presence of the whole Trinity in its processes.

Besides, the three functions are included in most religions. For instance, almost every religion has some sort of creation story, so which Creator are we discussing? Are we talking about the triune Creator, whom we name Father, Son, and Holy Spirit, and whose creation is understood in quite different ways from that in other religions?

To think that words for functions can distinguish the Godhead's three persons also dialectically vastly reduces the Trinity by separating the persons more than they ought to be—as if one person is not involved in the functions of another. In addition, to substitute functions for names diminishes God entirely by listing only three things that God does. Even more, the relationships of the persons are elided, and God is cheapened to jobs rather than elevated simply for who He is in intra-triune partnerships of unique particularity and intimate mutuality.

Surprisingly, this is not a new problem! Eunomius, a fellow bishop to Gregory of Nyssa (who lived about 330–395), thought that the biblical terms *Father*, *Son*, and *Holy Spirit* should be replaced with terms that were more philosophically precise. But Gregory responded that the scriptural terms "cannot be indiscriminately exchanged, as though what they designate will remain the same no matter what the vehicle."[18]

This is especially true primarily because the names *Father* and *Son* denote a relationship. To abandon them "does not simply jettison the biblical language"; it also eliminates "the idea of relationship which enters the ear with the words."[19] To dispose of the triune relationship is to discard explicitly what is central to God's character.

If, as I believe, Jesus gave us these names and urged us to use them, might it, finally, be a matter of spiritual pride and a rejection of our own proper relationship with God to abandon the Trinity's names?

TRINITY

It happened again this year! Once again a pastor used the illustration of three shoes—a hiking shoe, a business shoe, a sports shoe—to depict the Trinity. Last year he used the same example (only with five shoes!), and a five-year-old recognized the problem of Modalism, though of course she didn't call it that. Instead she exclaimed, "But you can't wear all five shoes at once!"

The ways in which the name *Trinity* is corrupted are legion. Throughout the history of the Church God's triunity has been a subject of vehement debate, the reason for some to be labelled "heretics," the source of antagonism with adherents of other monotheistic religions, and a topic vastly underestimated or over-explained with images that have serious flaws!

Some think the notion of "Trinity" is not very important— or not believable—since the word itself does not appear in the Scriptures.[20] However, numerous passages cite all three persons of the Trinity, though no text works out dogmatically how it is possible that they are all to be considered as one God.[21] As doctrinal historian J. N. D. Kelly insists, the presence of trinitarian language in the New Testament "is all the more striking because more often than not there is nothing in the context to necessitate it."[22]

How can we bring together these important biblical truths—that we worship *one* God (monotheism) and that Jesus the Christ is perceived as divine? As early as the 300s, Hilary of Poitier realized that God's "economy" of salvation (a phrase which "designates God's ordered self-disclosure in creation, in the history of Israel, and preeminently in the life,

47

death, and resurrection of Christ"[23]) necessitated a rethinking of the customary way of conceptualizing God.

For Hilary, "everything was transformed with the resurrection of Christ, and Thomas was the first to grasp the nature of the change" (79) when in encountering the risen Jesus he responded, "My Lord and my God!" (John 20:28–29). In *De Trinitate 7.3* Hilary offers this guide for thinking about God: "Though he is one he is not solitary" (78).

We should pay attention to Hilary, for one of the major corruptions of Trinity in our time is that so many churches concentrate on only one member of the Godhead—or perhaps two—or forget that all three exist and work in close relationship. As Catholic theologian Karl Rahner commented, "should the doctrine of the Trinity have to be dropped as false, the major part of religious literature could well remain virtually unchanged."[24]

For the past year I have been testing this comment by observing liturgies and literature and by asking participants at conferences, and these examinations have confirmed Rahner's hunch. Most congregational leaders admit that the churches they serve (and they themselves) emphasize one person or another, but have trouble paying sufficient attention to the fullness of God's trinitarian self. "Christian language, however, is resolutely tripartite."[25]

Some Pentecostal churches highlight the Holy Spirit, but rarely include the Father and Son. Evangelicals often sing about Jesus only or begin every single prayer with an address to the Father, but infrequently speak about the three persons together. Conference participants have even commented to me how unusual it has seemed to them when I pray with triune language or end a prayer to the Father with the ancient phrases, "through Your Son, Jesus Christ our Lord, who lives and reigns with You and the Holy Spirit, one God now and forever."

If we don't speak about the Trinity or think about God triunely, how can we live the trinitarian life? Another major corruption these days has arisen because the whole notion of "Trinity" has been thought to belong only to the realm of professionalized dogma construction. Indeed, in the history of the Church much effort has been expended to develop philosophical expositions of how the persons of the God-head relate (a topic labelled "the *immanent* Trinity" when that adjective is restricted to the closeness of the persons to each other and not to us). Conversation about the Trinity has thus been made abstract and removed from its practicality and life-transforming consequences. However, as Catherine LaCugna shows, "Trinity" has to do not only with the Bible, creeds, and liturgies, but it also relates to our understandings of what it means to be the Church (ecclesiology), of the sacraments, of grace and ethics and spirituality, and of ourselves as human beings (anthropology). For this to be the case in our Christian lives and churches, we must begin all our thinking with the triune nature of God in what is called the "economy" (*oikonomia*) of salvation, in God's self-communication in the person of Christ and the activity of the Holy Spirit.[26]

Of course, to know Trinity only by what God *does* would be insufficient, for God is more than what the Trinity does. However, who the Trinity *is* in God's self is an enigma so impenetrable and sublime, a truth infinitely beyond our ability to comprehend, a love so embracing and empowering, we do better to esteem than to explain. I find myself adoring instead of analyzing. As the church father Augustine remarked, "anyone who denies the Trinity is in danger of losing her salvation, but anyone who tries to understand the Trinity is in danger of losing her mind."[27]

The more I read the Scriptures, the more I notice what LaCugna calls "the one ecstatic movement of God outward by which all things originate from God through Christ in the power of the Holy Spirit, and all things are brought into union with God and returned to God" (223). Because God is intertwiningly three-personed, you and I can be enfolded into the divine embrace! As Henri Nouwen comments, we need the Trinity as a way to realize God's "increasing desire for intimacy. At first God was the God *for* us, our protector and our shield. Then, when Jesus came, God became the God *with* us, our companion and friend. Finally, when Jesus sent his Spirit, God was revealed to us as the God *within* us, our very breath and heartbeat."[28] Let that triune cascade of love bathe us and whirl us closer into God's heart!

This entry is twice as long as the others in this book, but Trinity simply overwhelms us once we start probing the mystery. Could we do better than to end by exulting with Dante?

> I began, "you wish that I manifest
>   here the essence of my ready belief,
>   and you ask also about the cause of it,
> and I answer, I believe in one God
>   alone and eternal who, not moved,
>   moves all the heavens with love and with desire, . . .
> And I believe in three eternal Persons,
>   and these I believe one Essence, so unified
>   and threefold that they agree with both *are* and *is*.
> On the profound, divine state of being
>   of which I speak now, the evangelical doctrine
>   many times puts the seal.
> This is the source, this is the spark
>   which afterward grows into a living flame,
>   and shines within me, like a star in heaven."[29]

FATHER

The title *Father* is often rejected as the proper name for the first person of the Trinity because it is thought to be patriarchal. Since many women have experienced mortifying abuse, particularly sexual, from their earthly fathers, some think that to use that name for God is to induce only bad memories, fears, hatreds, further suffering.

Many women with whom I have worked, however, are very glad to give up the name *father* for their abusive parent and to find instead a perfect Father, who cares for them with infinite compassion and upholds them in dignity and honor. The more we grasp the fullness of the biblical picture of our true divine Father, the more we can counteract the corruptions caused by human fathers' betrayals and treacheries.

In the First Testament, the term *Father* is used for God only 11 times, most notably in Isaiah 63–64, where it appears three times in correlation with the names LORD and *our Redeemer from of old*. Israel only rarely knew God with such an intimate name.

Jesus changes that in the New Testament, for He speaks of or to God with the term *Father* over 170 times,[30] most notably in Matthew and John. In Matthew Jesus speaks of "my Father" approximately 15 times, but He widens that out to include His listeners by saying "your Father" almost as many times.

In the Gospel of John, Jesus speaks of "my Father" about twenty times, but of "the Father" almost seventy—many times when He is saying such things as "I and the Father are one." In only one place does "your Father" occur, but it is in the intimate scene when the risen Christ tells Mary Magdalene at the empty tomb, "I am ascending to my Father and your

51

Father, to my God and your God" (20:17). In contrast to the First Testament, these occurrences suggest that our relationship with the divine Father is possible because Jesus is the Son.

Bishop of Constantinople Gregory of Nazianzus, 329–390, underscores this when he stresses that "Father is not a name either of an essence or of an action. . . . But it is the name of the relation in which the Father stands to the Son, and the Son to the Father." Those two names help us know that the Father and Son are of a common identity in their nature; the two persons share a common essence, but they are eternally distinct from each other in relationship.[31]

The last point is important, for since we have seen in the Son an exquisite care for women and great tenderness for them when they have suffered abuse by men (see, for example, John 8:1–11), then we can trust that the same is the character of the Father, whose *icon* the Son is (Col. 1:15). Furthermore, the Son is our High Priest, as the book of Hebrews so strongly illustrates, and as such He leads us through our worship into His own intimacy with His Father by the power of their Spirit.

Instead of bad memories, fears, hatreds, and suffering, then, our true heavenly Father gifts us with good hopes, assurances, love, and well-being. Moreover, since through His priestly intervention the Son makes known to us the first person of the Trinity as *"our* Father," He thereby welcomes us into the mutuality of the divine interrelationships that widens into our communal, interdependent dance with *all* God's children. Those who want to substitute a functional word like *Creator* for the name *Father* lose this particular intimacy—between the Son and the Father, between us as individuals and our Father, and between all the children of our heavenly Father.

We still are left with many questions impossible to answer, such as how the Father is father to the Son. But Jesus Himself has given us the name and invited us to use it. I trust His welcome into His own intimacy with His Father and rejoice to call God my Father, too. (It is ironic that the notorious "Jesus Seminar," known for its rejection of the authenticity of many of the sayings ascribed to Jesus by the Gospel writers, decided that the phrase *Our Father* was probably the only part of the Lord's Prayer that Jesus actually said.)

Some people want to substitute the word *Mother* for the first person of the Trinity. This, too, deviates drastically from the biblical testimony (and consequent doctrines of the faith) since *Father* indicates not essence, but relationship. Most simply, Jesus' *mother* was Mary.

There are many feminine images for God in the Scriptures, but never is God named *Mother*. *YHWH* is *like* a mother, in the fullness of divine compassion (Isa. 49:14–15)—and the Hebrew noun *racham* or "womb love" is used extensively in the First Testament to signify that mothering concern. Jesus compares Himself to a mother hen (Matt. 23:37, Luke 13:34) and uses a woman to illustrate God's searching for us in our lostness (Luke 15:8–10). But Jesus never called God His mother, since He called Mary that.

To call God *Father*, however, does not indicate gender, as if God the Father impregnated Mary in the virginal conception. Instead, Gabriel tells Mary that the Holy Spirit will come upon her and the power of the Most High will overshadow her (Luke 1:35). In the miracle of the conception, the Triune God accomplished an entirely new thing, beyond our gendered understandings.

Perhaps we would do best to leave it at that: an incomprehensible mystery of a divine birth, an undefinable relationship of Father and Son, an intertwining mutuality in the Trinity into which we are spurred by the Holy Spirit. What an indescribable gift: the Son invites us to call His Father ours!

It makes a world of difference for our prayers. When we think about God, we might use names like *the Almighty, the Eternal One, Creator, Sustainer of the Universe, Covenant Keeper, LORD, Ruler of the Cosmos, or God of all gods*. And in using such titles we risk turning the God who loves us into a mere abstraction. When we pray instead, will we, "with all the humility and directness and simplicity of childhood,"[32] revel in the proffered intimacy and say, "Father"?

HOLY SPIRIT

Isn't it peculiar that the Holy Spirit is either overemphasized or ignored?

Some church bodies focus entirely on the Holy Spirit and forget Christ's words that the Spirit points to Jesus (John 15:26, 16:14), who always leads us to His Father. Some individuals insist that they are guided by the Spirit, but are not willing to submit that conviction to the testing of the whole community. Some assemblies limit the gifts of the Spirit to certain manifestations and question the faith of those who don't share in specific practices, such as speaking in tongues. These same congregations usually fail to obey the apostle Paul's reminder that tongues should not be spoken in the public gathering unless there is an interpreter (1 Cor. 14:26–32).

On the opposite side are all the individual Christians and churches who ignore the Holy Spirit in multifold ways. Most often I reject the Spirit by not allowing the Comforter enough time to work in my mind, to enlighten me, convict me, console me, assure me (and thereby teach me to trust), sustain me, pray for me, or give me the right words to say or write.

In churches we quench the Spirit (1 Thess. 5:19–20) by not listening to *all* the voices in the community, especially such marginalized ones as the poor, the children and youth, the elderly, the handicapped—and in some communities, the women. We stifle the Intercessor by trying to control or at least manage everything ourselves, by not seeking the Kingdom of God first and trusting by the Spirit's power that everything else will then follow. We thwart the Spirit by not being open to the diversity of gifts with which the Distributor of charisms endows the Church.

Sometimes we spurn the Spirit by resorting to majority vote. Instead of conversing together as a community until we can honestly say, "we have reached consensus" and "it has seemed good to the Holy Spirit and to us" to proceed in a certain way (Acts 15:25, 28), we hasten the process, alienate each other, renounce the Spirit, and wield our own power to get our own way.

We seem not to believe that the Holy Spirit genuinely is and has been and will be the *Paraclete* that Jesus named. (This Greek word, now translated "Advocate," emphasizes the close companionship—the "called-alongside"ness—of the Spirit.) In connection with the Scriptures, we deny the Spirit by not trusting that the *Paraclete* inspired the biblical writers, accompanied the Church as it gathered its authoritative texts, and instructs us still as we hear and read.

Consequently, we renounce the Spirit when we do not let the Inspirer through the Word in biblical texts form our language and lives, when we are not attuned enough to the Spirit to let the Holy Guide direct our attitudes, speech, and deeds. We admire certain people who seem to be Spirit-filled, but do not comprehend that the Spirit's indwelling is a gift fully available to us all.

We also repudiate the Spirit when we do not submit to the Empowerer's gifting so that we might work out of God's strength rather than our own. How often we rely on our own skills, experience, understanding, or talent rather than letting the Spirit have full sway in our lives and deeds. Sometimes, conversely, we hide the Spirit's gifts and don't let them work through us for the well-being of the community or even ourselves.

We simply don't comprehend how prodigious are the Holy Spirit's works, how thorough could be the *Paraclete*'s indwelling, how strongly the Advocate desires to work in and through us for our good and the good of others. We need to join Basil the Great, Bishop of Caesarea, whose carefully elaborated treatise *On the Holy Spirit* (responding to the potent controversies over the third person of the Trinity in the years 325–381) declared that the Spirit's "works are ineffable in majesty, and innumerable in quantity."[33]

We need to ponder more earnestly what the Scriptures reveal about the activity of the Spirit as the work of God and then more unremittingly cry, "Come, Holy Spirit, come!"

Awesome

This might seem a funny entry in a book attempting to reclaim theological words for talking the walk, but it is a word that could be applied as a name for God's character, were it not so corrupted. In addition, the term is employed in some "contemporary" songs used for worship[34] and therefore ought to be considered here for its appropriateness in naming the Triune God.

I remember an animated discussion with my high school freshman English teacher over the word *awful*. I insisted on using the word *awe-full* to describe something so exalted as to arouse reverence, but she preferred I stick with the word's common spelling and its usage to designate something dreadful. We could have solved the debate easily by looking in the dictionary; for the word *awful* my old *Webster's New World Dictionary* (Second College Edition) lists as its first definition "inspiring awe; highly impressive." Not until its fourth entry does the dictionary supply this definition most frequently assumed, it seems, in idiomatic English: "very bad, ugly, unpleasant."

I lost the debate that day in class; the teacher had the final word. I remember, though, being deeply troubled beyond the dispute. It seemed to me (at age 14) that a really vital perception was being lost—the sense that something, someone, was higher than we. I longed to verbalize awe-full-ness; my teacher instead made class awful.

I've thought of that adolescent encounter frequently as I hear teenagers apply the related word *awesome* to clothes and food, to music and cinematic effects, and as a conversation-gap-filler similar to "mmm" or "like." The word is so overused for anything and everything that when people sing, "Our God is an awesome God," the song seems to trivialize the Awe-full One and put the Trinity on the same level as toothpastes and togs.

In a society characterized by "the humiliation of the word,"[35] in which we use words like *extraordinary* and *stupendous* to describe laundry soaps, what words do we have left to express breathtaking grandiosity? As our culture has worked hard to establish equality among persons, we have somehow put God into that parity and have gradually reduced our sense that this is **GOD** we are talking about.

It was, to be sure, an inevitable pendulum swing. Our forebears emphasized reverence and fear of the transcendent God to such an extent that a drive toward God's immanence was an unavoidable necessity. We seem somehow unable to keep the dialectical tension of God's exaltedness and humility, of the Trinity's distance from us and closeness to us, as an indispensable adhesion.

Might the prevalence of the expression "awesome!" suggest a hidden longing for some sort of transcendence?[36] Have we failed so badly to give our children and our world a vision of the One Who is, all at the same time,

immortal, invisible, God only wise,

in light inaccessible hid from our eyes,

most blessed, most glorious, the Ancient of Days,

almighty, victorious"?

"Thy great name"—how *do* we praise it?

PART II

WHY DO
HUMAN BEINGS
AND THE WORLD
NEED GOD?

BROKENNESS

It's a typical experience. Just now as I tried to print a writing project, something went inexplicably wrong. The printer started spitting out pages containing only one word per line. I tried frantically to stop it, but no commands worked. It kept going until the tray ran completely out of paper—about one hundred pages of sentences marching down the paper one word at a time.

Then my computer began screaming at me—a long shriek that did not end until I shut it off. Its shriek was matched by my own despairing cry to God, "Help me, help me!" I'm a computer illiterate, visually and mechanically impaired, totally incapable of fixing things, and alone in the house.

After more cries, a cup of tea, feeble prayer, and silent pondering, I fiddled with a few things in the project file and tried again—this time commanding only two pages to be printed. That worked fine, but, when I attempted to print the next fifteen, the paper jammed in the tray, tore when I sought to retrieve it, and left part of itself stuck somewhere in the dark recesses of the printer.

I'm equally stuck. Perhaps my husband can dislodge the paper when he gets home (since he's at least mechanical, though even less computer literate).

I'm caught more deeply, however. I'm stuck in a world that doesn't work right, where people get hurt, lives get frazzled, the land and water and air get damaged.

I'm even more stuck in my self. Though I'd love to be calm, patient, and wise about everything I've *tried* to learn, I always find myself anxious, cranky or angry, incapable of mastering important things, and irritatingly handicapped.

It's even worse when I'm with people. I don't say what I wish I could say. What I do say I later regret. I find myself peeved, judgmental, nasty, or, perhaps worst of all, unconcerned about others.

And as for loving God? I'm not doing very well right now. Couldn't God intervene so that I don't waste my time in such messes? Couldn't the Spirit empower me to fix things? Couldn't there be some remedy for all the ways that life goes wrong?

Some people these days like to use the word *brokenness* to summarize all the things I've been describing in these two pages, but that word has been terribly corrupted by being used as a way to escape responsibility for the deeper problems noted above, which previously were called "sin." Sometimes "brokenness" is used to reject the notion that there is evil in the world, or to ignore what's more wrong with such things as technology than that they simply malfunction frequently, or to dismiss any notion that there are other spirits in the world beyond the human.

If everything that goes wrong is simply because of "brokenness," why can't we fix it? Who ever came up with the idea that human beings are good? Who ever could think that the world is as it should be? Who ever could not realize that there is deep alienation in the universe? Who ever thought that the meager word *brokenness* was sufficient to name the mess we're in?

Maybe we should let the word go back to describing the state of such things as teacups.

DECADENCE

Why would restaurants name a dessert, "Chocolate Decadence"? Why do we corrupt the word *decadence* by turning it into a source for snickering that we've gotten away with eating something really not good for us or by using it to woo us into feeling good about breaking our dieting rules? We corrupt the word *temptation* in the same way. It has become almost a source of pride to fall to it!

It seems that almost all advertising is meant to make us feel good about indulging ourselves. What kind of people is that forming us to be?

The word *decadence* originally denoted a decline in morals or a deterioration of behavior. Do we use it to name a particular chocolate confection because we can't totally submerge our conscious awareness that to eat it would be to do harm to our body? Then doesn't such a title, luring us to indulge in the very thing that we know is not good for us, multiply our sin (if we give in to the temptation), for we do not eat to our destruction out of ignorance?

Why do we want to hurt ourselves so?

SIN

It has been popular recently to reject or at least to ignore the word *sin*. Why don't we talk about "sin" anymore? It is, as has been said, the only theological doctrine that can be readily seen in the daily newspaper.

The contemporary reticence to acknowledge sin is partly due to the thought that it's merely an incorrect action, the trifling result of a bad choice, a common mistake, or the result of our (destructive) upbringing, and not a deeply rooted problem.

Another reason for the corruption of the word *sin* by (not-so-benign) neglect these days is that a supreme value of our times is "tolerance." We fear to name anything as sin because we will be "guilty" of the ultimate of sins, "judgmentalism." (See "Self Esteem" below.)

A presupposition for tolerance is the corrupted idea that all things—including values, beliefs, words, and actions—are equal. That might seem like a truthful hypothesis at first glance, but it could readily be tested if I'd clobber you. You would probably find that action less than good (or questionable at least), but would we go so far as to call it "sin"?

To name something "sin," there must be some rule or basic moral law against which it is a violation. Or there must be some ordering, contrary to which we rebel (in thought, word, or deed). Or there must be some acknowledged evil in which we collaborate. Or there must be some specific legislation against which we are criminals. Or there must be some damage done, of which we are the perpetrators. Or there must be some relationship that we have *broken* (a word which ought not to be corrupted by weakening the violence of the rupture).

Beneath these forms of sin is the deeper issue, the root problem that we are initially so prone to these choices and behaviors. Have we a sinful nature? Are we, since birth, *sinners*?

Most dictionaries list both the actual deeds of disobedience or violation and the nature that gives rise to such offenses as the two fundamental meanings of the word *sin*. I think that it is more helpful to separate those two into "sins" and "sinfulness," for it is the horrendous predicament of our sinful nature from which we must be delivered before we can really understand the particulars of the sinning behaviors.

Let's begin by including the words *sin* and *sinful* in our language once again so that we face the double problem more squarely. Each of us has to confess that we are prone to sin and that we do sin more often than we admit—even if only by partaking of Chocolate Decadence.

CONFESS, CONFESSION

In worship services across the denominational spectrum I encounter corruptions of "confessions" that say things like "we are not able to love our neighbors" or "we do not treat our neighbors [or ourselves!] well." The first sample sounds almost like it's our Creator's fault that we have wronged our neighbors because we weren't made capable of doing better, and the second downplays how violent is the evil we have done to others by *sinning* against them.

Cornelius Plantinga's superb book aimed at recovering our sense and the language of sin parodies modern confessions with these examples: "Let us confess our problem with human relational adjustment dynamics, and especially our feebleness in networking" or "I'd just like to share that we just need to target holiness as a growth area."[1]

On the opposite side of the corruption spectrum are confessions that leave us in the depths of despair because we hear no specific, direct word of forgiveness. The point of acknowledging our sin is not to make us feel terrible, but to free us, by means of absolution, from that grievous haunting of guilt. A lot of people in our society walk around with huge burdens of remorse because they've been so busy euphemizing their sins that they haven't really faced them, admitted their responsibility and the depths of their sinfulness, and gotten rid of the encumbrance in the freedom of gracious deliverance.

We confess because we are invited to. Grace precedes it, grace makes it possible, and grace forgives what we acknowledge. Then, because we are liberated, grace works ever more thoroughly in us to keep us from the same misdeeds, offenses, violations, rebellions, faults, and vices.

Our church services need confessions something like this:

> Almighty God, we confess that we are in bondage to sin and cannot free ourselves. We have sinned against you in thought, word, and deed, by what we have done and by what we have left undone. We have not loved you with our whole heart; we have not loved our neighbors as ourselves. For the sake of your Son, Jesus Christ, have mercy on us. Forgive us, renew us, and lead us, so that we may delight in your will and walk in your ways, to the glory of your holy name. Amen.[2]

What a great confession! It's thorough enough to catch me every time, strong enough so that I know how deeply I've sinned, general enough so that no one can escape its power. It's a terrible bondage, this sin problem. The only way out is deliverance, liberation, forgiveness!

VICTIMS

Perhaps the strongest evidence of human sin in our time is that so many people in the world are victims of prejudice, cruelty, injustice, violence. For example, children are the victims of physical, mental, emotional, and sexual abuse—not only in more obvious and odious ways, but also in infrequently discerned, immediately or eventually destructive ways, such as when they aren't spurred to learn or don't have decent schools; when they have television (or nothing) as baby-sitters; when their natural curiosity is stifled or they're overloaded with "activities" which squelch creativity and playfulness; when they cannot get adequate nutrition or medical care.

The atrocities against persons throughout the world are myriad: women are raped; the poor not only can't eat, but also don't understand the systems that keep them entrenched in poverty; two-thirds world nations are the victims of the powerful who exploit their resources and strangle their local customs and cultures with the ubiquity of mass media and massive commodifications; violence waged with the "advances" of technology harm the innocent directly and indirectly by destroying infrastructures; Palestinian targets of the Israeli occupation and its bulldozing, shelling, curfews and other restrictions, and wall building see no hope for any future[3]; markets commandeered by the affluent leave no options for unschooled craftspeople; the healthy ignore the horrific dimensions of the AIDs crisis; the people behind the outrageous national and global statistics of disparities between the rich and poor are often excluded from the comfortable pews of our churches or from our supposedly Christian minds. The list of ways that those of us with the ability to read this book burden others—even though our oppressions might be unintentional or unconscious—is endless.

In response, some contemporary theologians say we have to give up the Christian message of a suffering and crucified Christ as hopelessly inadequate or cruelly insensitive. But it is a corruption to think that victims aren't also sinners, even though the primary incipient message of the Gospel for them is more appropriately that Jesus understands their suffering and is with them in it.

A larger corruption is to excuse the sins of victims (as a permitted response to their terrible situation) rather than holding them accountable for their misdeeds (even though their wrongs seem to be less virulent than those done to them). As Martin Luther taught, unbelief is the greatest sin—and for that we all need forgiveness.

A corruption of one's position as a casualty of injustice that frequently ensues in our world is that former victims in turn oppress new victims (a process readily seen as Israel reacts to its own horrendous experience of the Holocaust by choosing violence powerfully waged against Arab neighbors in order to "secure" its "safety"). Of course, it is humanly almost impossible to respond to one's victimizers with love and forgiveness, but the gifts of God's grace and mercy are encompassing enough to equip victims to respond, as Jesus did, with a greater power than violence.

A very common corruption in wealthy nations is to lose one's sense of proportion and claim to be a "victim" when one suffers only minor inconveniences or personal slights or injuries. The woman given a friendly wink (not consciously done as sexual harassment) ought not to place herself in the same category as women savagely raped by enemy soldiers. Or, as was an actual case, a person shouldn't fabricate the right to sue a fast food company for an enormous sum of money because the coffee was too hot. The many kinds and cases of legal actions over trifles which clog genuine justice in the world seem to be multiplying these days almost as fast as the true cries (often unheard) for redress.

To avoid all the corruptions of suffering, we must make careful nuances. We start with the Good News of the Trinity's attributes (Part I) and actions (Part III) as a story large enough to meet all needs.

Those who suffer in minor ways must deny themselves the self-pitying that leads to overstatement of one's troubles and hardness of heart toward both those who cause their petty distresses and those who are real victims of negligence, exploitation, torture, persecution.

Those who truly suffer must resist their tendency to wallow in their victimization. The Gospel can bequeath the right kind of power for them to find freedom in, and sometimes from, their oppressive situations.

Those who observe others' suffering have no excuse merely to "let the Gospel take care of the victims." Each person of whatever means can be involved in steps toward overcoming the world's various tyrannies that create victims.

Neither side—those who suffer more or less, those who cause others' suffering less or more—dare excuse their respective misdeeds, for, indeed, all have sinned and come short of the glory of God. Perhaps some of the wrongdoing could be eliminated if victims and oppressors learned how appropriately to speak the Gospel to each other.

Self Esteem

The prevailing wisdom (all too human!) is that we shouldn't talk about sin or confess sins because to do so makes us feel too bad; it pushes us into low self-esteem. When this faulty judgment invades churches, it corrupts their ability to offer to their members and their neighbors one of their best treasures, the gem of forgiveness for the crown of true identity.

The "Building Self Esteem" classes my husband was required to teach in the elementary school seemed to produce the opposite effect of their intended purpose. Deep inside, children did not believe that they were overwhelmingly lovable and good (as they were instructed to tell themselves). They knew they fought on the playground, disobeyed their teachers, disrupted class, and failed to do their homework. To tell ourselves that we are really not too bad does not actually build our self-respect or self-confidence, for then we add to our sense of culpability a bit of shame for our own hypocrisy.

The Church's greatest gift is forgiveness. It frees us from futile attempts to love ourselves on the basis of how pleased we are with what we are becoming, how we think, speak, and behave. If our self esteem is based on those qualities, we will surely be disappointed, for the good that we would, we can't do, and the evil that we don't want to do, we find ourselves doing. Romans 7 is everyone's experience.

But forgiveness frees us for the eschatological Joy[4] of Romans 8, the present and eternal confidence that there is no condemnation for us in Christ Jesus—a very good basis for genuine self esteem.

Self esteem can't be built by ignoring our sins; it can only be delivered by authentic escape from them.

THE FALL

I called for small group discussions and gave the clergy conference registrants a question to ponder so that I would have a few minutes to try to figure out how to proceed. I was so taken aback by one participant's remark that I couldn't think what to do next. He had attacked my views as too pessimistic about the nature of the world and ourselves; his objections culminated in the insistence that "the Fall" was progress.

That was a new twist on the old repudiations of the narrative in Genesis 3. Most deride the story simply as a fable or question its "historicity." Some agree that it makes a good point, but wonder if the Fall was so extensive as theologians for centuries have claimed. But I'd never heard before the conviction that the Fall was *progress*.

Can we really call it "progress" when we directly disobey a command and fracture our relationship with the God who made all things and yet wants to be in intimate conversation with us? Why is it that we, like Eve and Adam, are so prone to disobey because we are unable to tolerate mystery?[5]

Other corruptions of the doctrine of the Fall include laying the blame solely on God's enemy, the devil, or solely on the woman (a blaming directly related to the odious sin of patriarchal oppression of women). Sometimes God is indirectly accused for being the one who created the "tree of knowledge" in the first place or because the Creator gave (non-robotic) human beings freedom for good and evil.

None of these are very careful readings of the biblical narrative in Genesis 3!

Long ago I learned from Dietrich Bonhoeffer a more faithful reading of the text.[6] Bonhoeffer recognized that the root of our trouble lies in human beings' wrong use of the freedom we've been given, for we use it to try to be like God (or *the* god of our own small world). We keep choosing not to be utterly dependent upon God.[7] We continue to make choices that elevate us above our creatureliness and then we transgress the limits that God's grace has put upon us.[8]

We do this every time we question whether God really meant a certain command for us. We wonder, would a good God make such demands? We start to judge God's word rather than ardently hearing and doing it. We try to create our own "better" lives. The last thing we want is to *need* the Creator.

EVIL

All the ways people like to weasel out of admitting the existence of evil in the world are quite interesting! The Stoic types believe that we can draw up resources from inside ourselves to keep anything from bothering us. Evil to them is a figment of our imaginations, which ought to be kept better in check.

Others acknowledge the possibility of evil but accuse those of us who stress its existence of being extremists or pessimists. Some, instead, just give in to its prevalence and resign themselves to its perniciousness because, after all, there is nothing we can do about it since it is too pervasive for our feeble attempts at change to make much difference.

But perhaps the worst corruption is to use the existence of evil as a reason to judge God. And we are *so good* at judging God.

We say such things as "How could a good God allow such suffering in the world?" or "in my life?" Then there is the question, "Why is there so much evil in the world in the first place?" with its companion complaints, "God must not be very good to allow evil in the world" or "God must not be powerful enough to stop it."

All of these are ways to escape our own human responsibility. Dietrich Bonhoeffer recognized that such questions and complaints as those in the previous paragraph assume that we could "go behind" our own existence as sinners and, unclouded by sinful confusions and assumptions, *know* God's answers. But we are chronic (and stubborn) sinners and part of a world enmeshed in the consequences of universal sin.

Our questions suggest that we'd really rather make something or someone else responsible.[9]

We are not God! If we could be like God, "Wholly Other" and able to "get behind" our tainted human existence, I'm sure we would be totally satisfied with the answers we would know. And would there be any evil then to explain?

ORIGINAL SIN

The doctrine of "Original Sin" is usually corrupted because we try to figure out why it exists—is it passed on, many used to think, by sexual intercourse?—instead of recognizing its manifestations in our daily lives. We believe that we are basically exceedingly good—didn't God announce that when human beings were created?—but somehow, for some inexplicable reason, we have to admit, we don't act like we expect we should be able to act. Too easily and too regularly we disappoint ourselves. What is wrong?

It seems to me that we would do best to think about original sin not in terms of its cause, but of its ultimate result. This is named for us in Romans 5:12: "just as sin came into the world through one man, and death came through sin, and so death spread to all because all have sinned," therefore, death (q.v.) exercises dominion over us all unless we are set free from it by the enormous gift of grace in Christ Jesus.

Perhaps, rather than arguing about whether there really was an Adam and Eve and whether we are all guilty because of those persons, we should recognize that we do not come into life with a clean slate. We bear the imprint of the sins of our forebears.

For example, if our parents were raised by stern, disapproving ancestors themselves, it is less likely that their basic attitude of child-raising will be one of constant affirmation and acceptance—even if they earnestly desire to act in that way. In other words, we *have* a past.

Garry Wills remarks,

we are hostages to each other in a deadly interrelatedness. There is no "clean slate" of nature unscribbled on by all one's forebears. . . . At one time a woman of unsavory enough experience was delicately but cruelly referred to as "having a past." The doctrine of original sin states that humankind, in exactly that sense, "has a past."[10]

To emphasize original sin is not to be a pessimist (someday I hope to write on the corruptions of that term and of the idea of "Reality"), but to acknowledge with unveiled consciousness that we are seriously fractured from the beginning, that we cannot be whole no matter how hard we try. Our *nature* is to make ourselves God, so we all share in this "original" sinfulness and its result in death. We are very good at self-deception (see Jeremiah 17:9); we have plenty of defense mechanisms to keep ourselves safe. As psychologist/spiritual director David Benner quips, to deceive ourselves about the true state of our reality is our "default option."[11] We are overwhelmingly incapable of facing the truth of our own alienation from ourselves and from God and from others.

We are not overcome by this sinfulness, of course, because God has done something about it, as we shall see in Part III of this book. However, we take God's actions too lightly if we don't recognize first how desperate we are for grace.

It is a tricky dialectical tension. Some people are overwhelmed by sin and need to be enfolded in the rich embrace of God's gracious love. Some people, on the other hand, are blithe about sin and need deeper instruction in its pervasiveness. The latter seems to predominate in our generation.

We have to remember the battle in which we are presently engaged concerning our sinful nature. Early in the history of the Church, Irenaeus fought against Gnostics who insisted that materiality was evil, created mistakenly by some sort of lower deity. Consequently, Irenaeus concentrated on creation's goodness, whereas Augustine a few centuries later dealt primarily with Pelagians, who had an overly optimistic attitude about the human ability to remedy our human problems since, they insisted, God wouldn't ask us to do something we're not capable of doing.[12]

Is our present society morally crippled (as the Roman society surrounding Augustine) or overwhelmed with guilt, as were many of our forebears? Literature available in bookshops might suggest an answer to that question, as do the daily newspaper and the percentage of movies that are rated "Not Suitable for Children" (not because of the intellectual level required).

We have a past and a surrounding cultural ethos, and both are deadly. We need to appreciate the extent of its destructiveness, lest we take for granted the graciousness of God (see Part III).

We cannot discover the fullness of life (and what a gift it is) unless we know how dead we are. The doctrine of original sin reminds us that we were dead before we were even born, lest we think we can somehow get the chance to fix things.[13]

CLASS

Today it hammered my soul, the word *class*. We don't usually talk about it in North America. We blame on race distinctions problems that really originate in class disparities, and we fail to recognize that a primary cause of a great proportion of class disparities lies in generations of unequal treatment of the races.[14]

In general, this word is corrupted by being ignored. I can accept insights about "class" intellectually, but struggle to deal with it morally.

When I was a child, class didn't seem to have much to do with me. My parents didn't have very much; our family was on the lower end of the economic scale (I thought!), at least compared with most of my classmates in primary school.

Radically exposed to poverty when our around-the-world college choir tour took us to India, however, I saw there deprivation and desperation unimaginable in my hometown, nestled as it was in the midst of good-earthed farms. I hadn't felt rich before—didn't I have to work three or four jobs along with college courses and music practices to finance that choir trip (since all proceeds from our concerts supported the indigenous churches)? Encountering the starving inflamed me with a new devotion to feeding the hungry.

Since then, I've tried not to be rich. I purposely don't earn much; my husband and I try to give a lot away; we try to live simply.

But that last phrase betrays me. "Living simply" is an option only for the rich.

So I start up the endless rounds of answerless questions. If I weren't rich enough to afford these tools and this place to work, how could I write books that produce royalties to divert to organizations that serve the needy? If I gave up all the trappings (and the substance) of my wealth, would I be able to do more to change the disparities of class?

But if I lived anywhere else, I wouldn't be alive anymore. Too many medical technologies and a certain measure of sanitation are constantly necessary to sustain my handicapped life. Should I give up those options of my affluence in order to identify more closely with the poor? What would God *expect* of me? What would God *want* from me?[15]

Once when I was leading a series of weekly Bible classes on Sundays, a participant complained, "You are always talking about giving for the sake of the poor. How much do we have to give?" I blithely replied, "More. The answer is always, 'More.'" But does the God who created beauty desire austerity? Don't we honor God by enjoying beauty—in art, music, lovely things?

Yes, beauty does not require opulence—it can be simple— but how do we draw the line? How do we distinguish between enjoying God's gifts and oppressing the poor?

It's not enough to be constantly haunted by such questions, or even to act on the few answers we can discern. We have to know and confess how caught we are (you've got class!) in injustice and follow blindly the One who came "so that those who do not see may see" (John 9:39).

FAME

It is a great temptation these days for churches, or preachers, or musicians (or anybody else for that matter) to want to be famous. We even have good motivations (partially)—we want to be influential for the sake of the Gospel.

But as philosopher Albert Borgmann once said (in a gathering of persons concerned about the effects of technology on Christianity and culture), "Fame is like chocolate mousse. It tastes so good that you gobble up the entire dishfull, only to discover that it was just air."

Far worse than the disappointment of the futility of fame is its destruction of our spiritual lives. The Psalmist knew his stuff when he wrote,

> A craving seized them in the wilderness,
>   and they put God to the test in the desert.
> He gave them what they asked,
>   but sent leanness into their soul.[16]

As my beloved spiritual director once said, "Unless we are faithful with our inner work, our outer work will suffer." Lord, rescue us from fame, lest its air smother us into leanness of soul.

Guilt

Guilt has several corruptions, expanded by our society's ethos.

Sometimes we are truly guilty, but refuse to admit it. We have done something wrong and deserve blame or punishment. (Perhaps instead we hire a really expensive, high-powered lawyer who can win the trial and get us off the hook, free!)

Sometimes we corrupt guilt by *feeling* guilty and painfully reproach ourselves when we have not really done the wrong that we imagine. We punish ourselves even if we do not deserve blame for the particular offense we have invented.

Our society amplifies those two corruptions by not distinguishing between true guilt and false guilty feelings and consequently by insisting that all feelings of guilt should be banished. We ought not to feel bad about ourselves, our culture says; we shouldn't harm our own "self-esteem" (q.v.) that way.

Of course, in truth, feeling guilty about our guilt is a good thing. It leads to remorse, repentance, confession. It opens up the possibility for genuine forgiveness, restoration of relationships, reformed behavior.

One of the great gifts with which the Church is endowed by God is that it can be a community of compassionate caring to help those who are truly guilty acknowledge the extent of their sin and experience forgiveness and renewal and to help those who falsely feel guilty to be set free from their mistakenly-burdened conscience.

Don't tell me not to feel bad about myself. Instead, spur me to confession and assure me I'm forgiven or embrace me in the fullness of God's love and approval.

Opinion

The value of "Opinion" in our society has been so corrupted as to have taken on sinful proportions. Opinions have become our personal gods or, more accurately, the proof that we are our own gods. They signify our autonomy, a massive leveling of all convictions, the abandonment of all standards, the elimination of truth.

It drives me nuts! I have tried to talk with certain pastors about the historic faith, about doctrines upon which the Church has agreed for centuries, and the response is always, "Well, that's your opinion; we're entitled to our own."

Certainly there are truths beyond opinion. Wouldn't everyone agree that a loving marriage is better for us than hatred and distrust? Don't we all think generosity is preferable to stinginess? Doesn't the world need peacemaking and justice more than violence and oppression?

Once, a few years ago at a youth convention, a lovely young lady came earnestly to talk with me. She asked me what I thought about a certain matter in sexual ethics. I answered her with the most careful biblical reading and ethical nuancing I had gained in years of training.

She responded, "Well, I just wanted to know your opinion."

"That wasn't my opinion," I replied. "If I had given you my opinion, it would have been the opposite because I really would like to escape these biblical truths and say what pleases everybody. I tried to tell you as faithfully as I could what all my studies have discerned God is saying. That's much more sound, more reliable, more eternally true than my measly opinion."

She looked at me in shock. How could anyone question the importance of personal opinion? How could anyone give an answer different from her own private feelings? Is there really such a thing as public truth?

Yes, there is. And truth's name is God.

PRIDE

Most of us aren't really interested in terribly sordid sins of the flesh or in abhorrently abominable deeds of cruelty—though we must remain very wary, for, as we all know, "Pride goes before destruction, and a haughty spirit before a fall" (Prov. 16:18). Proper pride of character (which is, to remember that we are the children of God) can keep us from these (or any which we think are lesser) sins, whereas pride in ourselves as "good people" can prevent the watchfulness that might keep us from sinning.

More than that, it turns out that pride is perhaps personally the most destructive of sins because it is connected to our human desire for independence, our "normal" ambition to assert ourselves. Can we really learn to relinquish that "self" and become thoroughly dependent on God's Spirit to direct our life? Sometimes we need the sharp jolt of disillusionment to realize how miserably unable to "fix" ourselves we are.

As Oswald Chambers wrote in his best-selling *My Utmost for His Highest,* "Beware of refusing to go to the funeral of your own independence."[17] Similarly, Karl Barth said, "For those to whom God wills to be all in all, God strips everything else."[18]

To escape our arrogance and to become totally God's won't just cost us a little—it will cost us *everything* of our "self," for as Jesus said, "If any want to become my followers, let them deny themselves and take up their cross and follow me" (Matt. 16:24).

It is our pride that keeps us clinging to our "self," and it is our trusting of ourselves that keeps us from depending upon God. How can we learn afresh each day that the only reason to take up a cross is to die on it?

JUDGMENT

Our society has corrupted the word *judgment* because of its loathing of anything resembling the severe judgmentalism of former eras. Furthermore, somehow people have gotten the impression that to talk about sin and judgment is to deny the valid achievements of our present culture or individual persons.

Many people take the words of Jesus, "Do not judge" (Matt. 7:1), without considering the entire context in which our Lord criticizes our ignorance of our own sinfulness and the hypocrisy that makes us judgmental. Similarly, Luke 6:37 includes "do not judge" in a passage focusing on condemnation and lack of forgiveness, in contrast to the mercy of the heavenly Father. Somehow, John 7:24, a text accepted as written by Jesus' best friend, gets entirely forgotten, and it is the text which distinguishes types of judgment. What is forbidden is judging "by appearances," but judging "with right judgment" is authorized.

A worse corruption entails not believing that God rightly judges. Our present society likes to say, "God loves you," without any consideration that God loves us *in spite of* our sinfulness and not because we are lovable. Furthermore, the idea that "God loves you" is usually conveyed without any sense of how much it costs God to love us. Finally, those who hallow this corruption forget that God's love *involves* judgment, for God certainly spends our lives demonstrating triune love for us through divine judgment of us. Remember, after all, that God "disciplines us for our good, in order that we may share His holiness" (Heb. 12:10b). As professor of preaching

Thomas Long stresses, "I believe that God loves us so much that God will judge us."[19]

Perhaps if, for the sake of true love, we must judge another person with pains-takingly careful mercy and compassion, we do it rightly only if we believe and express the conviction that God is judging us both.

SATAN (OR THE DEVIL)

Even the brilliant nineteenth-century poet Johann Wolfgang von Goethe (whose religious beliefs were quite nebulous) acknowledged the existence of a cunning, clever, deceptive, majestically self-aware Satan, "the power that negates." In his *Faust*, Goethe pictured him (or his servant) with the shady character Mephistopheles. (Good grief: what pronoun do we use for Satan, who is definitely not a him or her and maybe not even an it? We'll have to use the conventional forms or use more of the biblical names.)

It's interesting to me that the wildly popular Harry Potter books describe the ultimate force of evil, Voldemort, in strikingly biblical terms. In one scene, in which Harry reacts angrily to the disbelief of his classmates concerning his encounters with the one they call (out of fear) "You-Know-Who," his good friends Hermione and Ron try to calm him down and assure him that they're on his side. When Harry apologizes, Hermione reminds the two boys that their headmaster Dumbledore had warned them of the evil one's tactics. At the end of the previous school year he had said, "'His gift for spreading discord and enmity is very great. We can fight it only by showing an equally strong bond of friendship and trust—.'"[20]

In contrast to these two examples from literature, today the existence of such an entity as the Devil or Satan is curiously corrupted from opposite sides. Some people dismiss the names and the entity as the product of an outdated cosmology that no one believes anymore. Contrarily, others turn the reality of Satan into an outmoded cosmology that any contemporary person shouldn't believe anymore.

The Bible does neither. It takes seriously the Devil—after all, Jesus battled Satan—but the Scriptures don't try to define Lucifer, locate the accuser in some three-story universe (of heaven, earth, and hell), or explain the diabolical one's existence. The superior power of evil is simply named, and the Prince of Lies' functions illustrated narratively.

Part of the confusions arise because usually the entire First Testament is ripped out of its historical context, a time when Hebrew writers disclosed evil but were not really able to name its source without sacrificing their utter monotheism, which emphasized that ultimately God was the source of everything.

Only after the Babylonian Captivity, when the Jews were exposed to Zoroastrianism and its dualism of equally-powerful agents of good and evil, do we actually see "Satan" used as a proper name and then only in 1 Chronicles 21:1 (compare 2 Sam. 24:1) and in Zechariah 3:1–2. At all other times, the word is used to mean "the accuser" and is written with the Hebrew article (*the* in English) as *ha-satan*. The word for "devil" is never used in the Hebrew texts.

In the New Testament the names *Devil* (as well as *the devil*) and *Satan* are used interchangeably, and in Revelation 12:9 and 20:2 both proper names are employed. Throughout, the Bible does not make Satan equal to God. C. S. Lewis recognized that there can be no opposite to God. Satan, rather, seems to be the antithesis to the great archangel Michael.

Why does all this matter? I think we make a serious mistake if we ignore the existence and destructive power of Satan. As many, including C. S. Lewis, have wisely noted, there are two mistakes to make about the devil—one to take him too seriously and the other to take him not seriously enough.[21] In faith I don't have to fear him, but I also don't have to be able to describe him to know that his dominance (and that of his minions) is being wielded in our messed-up world. British author Steve Turner calls Satan "the King of Twists," and we can easily point to myriads of ways in which words and stories are twisted, in which various powers of evil twist hearts and minds.[22]

I don't think our culture is so very much smarter than cultures that are considered more "primitive." For example, in Madagascar I experienced Christian communities who recognized the presence of Satan and other powers of evil in opposition to the work of the Gospel. Christianity there has flourished in part because those who follow Jesus have been able to cast out evil spirits and forces. Even in the U.S. I have experienced a physical battle with some sort of spirit or power of evil which was afflicting one of my university students and which finally departed only when I screamed, "Be gone, Satan, in the name of Jesus Christ."

On the other hand, some religious groups these days want to return to medieval descriptions of Satan and, consequently, develop pre-modern cosmologies vastly disproved by contemporary astronomy. These groups seem to know more than the Scriptures about the realities of evil and its perpetrators.

Globally-respected twentieth-century theologian Arthur Piepkorn offers a sane non-corruption. Quoting Martin Luther's morning prayer, "Let Thy holy angel be with me that the wicked foe may have no power over me," Piepkorn acknowledges his awareness that

> there is more to our universe than God and man and inanimate matter. My mysterious dual nature that stands in the doorway between the seen and the unseen creation puts me at the mercy not only of the beasts about me and the beast that lurks within me, but also at the mercy of the spiritual forces which are on the other side of the threshold and of which I have only vague intimations. Both Satan with his minions and the angels of light have been subjected in our time to a degree of over-anthropomorphization and over-objectivization which neither the data of the Sacred Scriptures nor my human experience enables me fully to control. But whatever and whoever the devil is and whatever and whoever the principalities and the princes of spiritual wickedness in the heavenly places may be, I am a potential victim of their malice and I need the help of beings of their own order. Similarly, whatever and whoever the angels may be, I look to them as ministering spirits that God sends forth to serve

for the sake of those who obtain salvation (Hebrews 1:14). This ultimately is comfort and encouragement for me. Even Satan is not God or a god; he is only a kind of angel and not the most powerful, for the angel called Michael vanquished him [Rev. 12:7–9].[23]

Why don't we take the devil as seriously as Jesus did—and then rest in His victory over him and all the other powers of evil?

PRINCIPALITIES AND POWERS

This subject is corrupted from two directions. There are those who delegate "Principalities and Powers" to the ashbin of "outdated cosmology"; on the other hand are those who equate (and thereby confuse) the principalities and powers with spirits or angels (which actually form an entirely separate category of words in the Scriptures). This latter group bloats its corruption by writing gruesome novels of attacks by flying forces, dressed out in medieval imagery.

We can think about the principalities more biblically if we remember the few, but diverse things we are told about them in the Scriptures. Most important, they are created by God for good (Col. 1:16).

However, they share in the fallenness of the world and must be treated so. It is ironic that many who admit that human beings have a sinful nature refuse to acknowledge that the powers, too, though created for God and good, share in the world's fallenness and wait with groaning for the recapitulation of the cosmos when God's kingdom is realized (Rom. 8:19–23). Left unguarded—by laws, wise resisters (see Eph. 6:10–20), societal customs, or other powers—the principalities *tend* to overstep their vocation and become gods in our lives (see 1 Cor. 8:4b–5).

The crucifixion of Jesus exposed some of the powers (Col. 2:15). Religious leadership was shown to be fallen when its communal clout was used to manipulate politics. Political institutions operated as oppressive powers when just laws about fair trials were violated. Money became the god Mammon as an unsuspecting but cooperative disciple was lured beyond false assumptions into betrayal. Notice that all three instances involved human people and forces larger than themselves.

These few details—and the complete lack of a definitive description or even definition of the powers—compel us to ask, then, not about the being or essence of the powers but about the functions of these humanly connected forces, carrying inordinate (supernatural) power. For example, why does money (Mammon) have such control over us?[24]

Lest we think the problem with money is simply personal sin, let's ask why, right now, it so controls the United States, its internal politics, its entire economy, its international policies—to the detriment of human relationships, the national common good, justice in the global community, and genuine peace in the world.

Furthermore, the various powers are usually interconnected. Why is so much money being spent throughout the world for war and war-making materials? Or, to point to other linkages, why has the U.S. economy continued to depend upon its citizens purchasing an ever-increasing amount of "new" and "updated" technological gadgets? Why do people spend escalating sums for health-enhancing supplies or weight-loss materials to offset the swell of fast food consumption? Why do marketing dollars swallow such a large portion of businesses' budgets?

Were about 120 Methodists wrong to send this letter to President George W. Bush?:

> It is with grieving hearts that we write publicly urging you to live faithfully the vows we share made at our baptisms and later affirmed. It is our judgment that some policies advanced by your administration give evidence of the spiritual forces of wickedness that exist in our world today.
>
> You have stated that the use of violence in a pre-emptive strike against the sovereign nation of Iraq would be to keep peace. This notion of redemptive violence is incongruent with Christ and his teaching. Following the Prince of Peace is by no means easy. It requires the courage to seek justice, the compassion to love kindness and the patient determination to walk humbly with God.[25]

When we consider why "things" just aren't as they should be, perhaps we would be wiser to believe the biblical insight that principalities and powers, created for the good of the world, share in universal "fallenness" and act outside of their proper vocation. Wouldn't our presidential policies and campaigns be less violent if we remembered that we are fighting not against "flesh and blood, but against the principalities, against the powers . . ." (Eph. 6:12, RSV)?

THE WORLD

Many of us who criticize the state of the world are accused of being negativists, pessimists, cynics, reactionaries, purists, and so forth. The fact is that we are realists—and I am a very hopeful one, at that. But the idea that the world is a problem has been corrupted because of the contemporary inability to understand this nuance: that criticizing elements of the world's condition does not mean that we are rejecting its whole existence or the very gifts that it offers.

The Bible is much more open to the good and the bad of the world. The word *world* is among the many terms that can have positive, neutral, or negative connotations in different settings. For example, the Gospel of John employs the word to emphasize God's gifts to the cosmos of love (3:16), salvation (3:17; 4:42), life (6:33, 51), and light (3:19; 8:12; 9:5; 11:9). The Pharisees complained that the raising of Lazarus caused such a stir that the world had "gone after" Jesus instead of trusting them (12:19). On the other hand, John's Gospel also discloses, the "world" did not know Jesus, needs its sin taken away (1:29), and is the place of those who reject him (8:23).

Maybe Martin Luther wasn't so far off when he labelled evil's sources as "the devil, the world, and my sinful flesh."

Perhaps Christians would live in a better relationship with the whole world if we loved it as thoroughly as God does and if we remained as committed as God is to set it free from its dominations and to restore it in the final recapitulation—and yet remained wary about the effects of "fallenness" and about the "principalities and powers" that tend to dominate it in the meanwhile.

95

HELL

The great U.S. minister to the Hague and to Russian courts, senator, secretary of state, president, and then representative to Congress, John Quincy Adams, knew part of the true meaning of the word *hell* when, as he stood against slavery, he wrote this in his diary for March 29, 1841:

> The world, the flesh, and all the devils in hell are arrayed against any man who now in this North American Union shall dare to join the standard of Almighty God to put down the African slave trade; and what can I, upon the verge of my seventy-fourth birthday . . .—what can I do for the cause of God and man. . . . Yet my conscience presses me on . . .[26]

That kind of courage and persistence are needed today for battles against the forces of hell.

Instead, a great percentage of people these days corrupt the biblical truth of "hell" by ignoring it. On the opposite side of the theological spectrum, many like to mis-accentuate its horrors with lurid and spectacular details. Oftentimes such people seem too eager to put others there, as if they had the right to wield such vengeance.

Another way to corrupt the word *hell* is to apply it too flippantly. I wonder if people have seriously thought of the consequences when they say such things as, "To hell with you." I know I have trivialized the word with such sentences as "This hurts like hell," at times when my multiple handicaps seem to gang up on me with crescendos of pain. The truth is, *nothing* except hell hurts like hell!

Perhaps many of our corruptions arise because we associate "hell" with a place, rather than a condition. We can easily dismiss the place as an imaginative depiction by ancient theologians.

The condition of hell is the greatest terror I can imagine—to be without God. Sometimes we put ourselves into this bondage now, and it leads to the deepest despair we can experience. How can we ever truly conceive of what it could mean to be eternally without God? And yet, the Bible insists that this is the judgment some people choose: to prefer the darkness to the presence of the one true Light (John 3:19).

C. S. Lewis illustrates types of this choice in his masterful *The Great Divorce*.[27] Throughout that book and the Bible before it these two important truths about hell become clear: God loves us too much to want us to wind up in any sort of hell, present or eternal, and God loves us too much to cram heaven down our throats.

EXCITING

Present-day medical practice has coined the diagnosis, "Attention Deficit Disorder," and it is true that for some this is a serious illness. For others, however, it is simply a correctable lack of self-discipline, the failure of parental guidance, the development of bad habits of overdosing on technological stimulations, or the result of personal or imposed choices to participate in everything without any sense of the body's need for balancing of activity with repose, solitude with community, and so forth. In these cases the "ADD" diagnosis gives us something else to blame.

One manifestation of the disorder in its culpable forms is the corruption of the word *Exciting*. These days everything has to be exciting. We move from one intense experience to another and expect the thrill level to continue escalating. Furthermore, for something to be "exciting," it usually has to be "new." These are but two words I could have picked to raise the issue of our cultural "need" for constant stimulation.

We can see the results of this depravity in a diversity of fields. Churches have to throw out everything they ever knew about worship so that each corporate experience of it can be new and exciting. One year I noticed in the newspaper "Churches" section that every single listing of Easter worship services except one used the word *Exciting*. What made those services so? In most cases, I would guess, the motivation for that word choice was not the presence of the Risen Christ in our midst. If it were so, I think other words choices would have been more appropriate.

Similarly, elementary educational materials and programs must always be new and exciting. As an experienced teacher, my husband recognized that most of those were not at all improvements for the sake of better teaching and genuine learning. He distrusted the word *exciting*; he had discovered that usually if the word was used, what it advertised was not.

I make this harsh judgment not primarily for the sake of raising and teaching children or to improve churches' sense of worship (though in some instances perhaps better attention to our words might be helpful), but rather for my own sake. I need to ponder the problem of needing stimulation. I seem to have an attention deficit disorder when I pray.

We "X" somebody to dis-hire, disown, distance,
   just like we cross off a job on our list.
A yesterday ago an X could mean your name
   and demonstrate life against the limitations
                         of innocent ignorance.
Your X said you existed, were a person, mattered.

Now X means a generation—
     lost, some think,
        or at least,
           struggling to find a way, Xers admit,
               to survive "Life after God"—
   but usually lumped together anyway,
         to be analyzed,
            separated from other generations,

            abandoned

by fast-climbing parents,

   criticized for their entertainments,

   condemned,

   convicted for their confusion
          (or should the preposition be *in* or *by*?)

If X could be redeemed (by One whose name it begins)
     and if we took back
         (by crossing ourselves)

X

all those crossed off
            by labels
                by wars
                                    (outward or inward)
        by others' luxuries or prejudices
                        or our own,

then the hungry would be fed
    and the home-less would be taken in
                to ours
and the lonely would be sheltered
    and a generation would become persons
        and the separations would cross into
                                    wholeness

    and the bottom feet of X would be grounded again
and the arms upraised

in praise.

DEATH

At funeral homes we hear the worst corruptions in how we think about death. When my cousin died unexpectedly and left her husband bereft and struggling alone to keep the farm afloat, I wanted to slug those who said, "Oh, it was God's will for her to die." Similarly, a mother reported to me her anger when her infant died and well-meaning Christians said, "God needed your baby more than you did." She wanted to respond, "then why didn't God just create a new one for Himself?"

How could people be so heartless and treat death as less than the enemy that it really is?

Contrarily, some corrupt the truth of death by making it more than it really is. These are the people who conceive of death as punishment, as only a source of despair, as defeat for the medical practice charged to care and not necessarily to cure, as hopeless finality.

It seems that every corruption we could name makes either too much or too little of death.

The Scriptures say that it is an enemy, but they also say that it has lost its sting.

It is a universal enemy, for the death ratio is the same: one per person. However, it has lost its sting: Jesus Christ has defeated death by passing through it and coming out on the other side, the first fruits of a whole new creation.

Only when we keep these two truths in balance can we deal rightly with death. It is an enemy; it robs us of loved ones, takes them before they've fulfilled their potential.

But it has lost its sting: our loved one is freed from pain. An old person is eager to "go home." The feeble are delivered from their earthly debilitations.

102

Humanly, we think we can balance the truths of death as an enemy and death losing its sting more easily the more full the life of the dead one was. Spiritually, however, they are easiest to balance when we know with assurance that Jesus grieves with us in our loss and that Christ's Resurrection is the sure hope that death is not the final story. Thanks be to God![28]

Can we discover this secret exultation, expressed by the early Christian preacher, John Chrysostom?:

> If any person is devout and loves God, let him come to this radiant triumphant feast.
> If any person is a wise follower, let him enter into the joy of his Lord, rejoicing. . . .
> Therefore, all of you [workers from the first hour to the last], enter into the joy of your Lord.
> Rich and poor together, hold high festival. . .
> The table is full; all of you, feast sumptuously.
> The calf is fatter; let no one go away hungry.
> Enjoy the feast of faith; receive the riches of God's mercy.
> Let no one bewail his poverty, for the fullness of the kingdom is revealed.
> Let no one weep for his iniquities, for forgiveness shines forth from the grave.
> Let no one fear death, for the savior's death has set us free.
> He who was held prisoner by death has annihilated it.
> By descending into death, he made death captive.
> He angered it when it tasted of his flesh. . . .
> It was angered, for it was defeated.
> It was angered, for it was mocked.
> It was angered, for it was abolished.
> It was angered, for it was overthrown.
> It was angered, for it was bound in chains.
> It received a body and it met God face to face.
> It took earth and encountered heaven.
> It took that which is seen and fell upon the unseen.
> O Death, where is your sting?
> O Grave, where is your victory?
> Christ is risen and you are overthrown.
> Christ is risen and the devils have fallen.
> Christ is risen and the angels rejoice.
> Christ is risen and life reigns.

Christ is risen and not one dead remains in the grave.
For Christ, being risen from the dead, is become the first
  fruits of those who have fallen asleep, and to him be
  glory and honor, even to eternity. Amen.[29]

Why then do we live so much as if death were the last
word—piling up our accomplishments, trying to build a legacy
by which we'll be remembered, attempting to grab every experience we can while we're able, entombed in fear of every
little ailment that leads us closer to death?

Just think how it would change us—and the world—if we
lived the eternal life God has already given us now! Why do
we live in so much death when it has been annihilated?

Part III

Actions
of God

Acts (of God)

For a period in biblical interpretation, scholars focused on the "Acts of God" as a way to get at texts, to organize systematic theologies, to discuss who God is. Of course it was a corruption. God is too sublime to be reduced to the divine acts; the Bible is too full of surprises to be systematized; texts are too multi-meaninged to be reduced to the actions alone. And even if we study the narrative of one of God's acts diligently, we can't comprehend all that it signifies throughout history, throughout the cosmos, throughout eternity.

We can look at what God has done only with humility, anticipating that God will constantly reveal to us new dimensions of the act's significance. As Philip Yancey summarizes from his interviews with Frederick Buechner, the latter profoundly trusts that "God is alive and present in the world," but he is not at all surprised "that God gives us only 'momentary glimpses into a mystery of such depth, power and beauty that if we were to see it head on, in any way other than in glimpses, I suspect we would be annihilated.'"

We corrupt the whole notion of God's interactions with history also by noticing them only in the dramatic interventions of global floods, mountain theophanies, tumbling city walls, fiery chariot snatches, startling resurrections, and magnetic preaching or emotion-hoisting music. Such a notion of "a God up in heaven who periodically dispatches a lightning bolt of intervention" fails to acknowledge that when God offers such sensational demonstrations of divine presence, "they usually follow years of waiting and doubt."

Buechner, through Yancey, suggests a quite different model, by which we fathom God's abiding presence "beneath history, continuously sustaining it and occasionally breaking the surface with a visible act that emerges into plain sight, like the tip of an iceberg." It doesn't take much spiritual training to "notice the dramatic upthrusts—Pharaoh certainly had no trouble—but the life of faith involves a search below the surface as well, an ear fine-tuned to rumours of transcendence."[1]

In this particular part of the book we will be trying to reclaim some words about God's acts, many of them the grand ones. But may our investigations of these words give us practice for the larger iceberg (holy fire) quest, the infinite adventure of discovering where and how God IS.

MYSTERY

We often speak of the way God works as "Mystery," but we corrupt that original New Testament word (*musterion*) if we dilute it with our experience of bright mystery stories that determine merely whether the butler or the maid dispatched the rich man's guest without poisoning his dinner companion. We might do a bit better if we look at the most clever of mysteries, something like a novel by the masterful Dorothy Sayers or G. K. Chesterton.[2] The works of these brilliant writers, both Christians, include extremely complicated puzzles, for which only one clue is discovered at a time, and often the clue completely shatters any previous theories the reader might have constructed. Eventually Lord Peter Wimsey or someone else figures the whole problem out, but the ending of the book still turns into more surprises that demand a rereading or at least leave the reader pondering for a long time.

Similarly but more intensely, with God and how God has rescued humanity and the rest of the cosmos, we never run out of clues. Each clue changes the picture—and, once in a while, we discover something (or, more accurately, something is revealed to us) that blows all our theories out of the water.

It will take us all eternity—and then some—to get the whole picture! But meanwhile the Bible, the cosmos, the Christian community, and the Spirit dwelling in our hearts keep giving us hints of the grandeur of God. Each bit of the mystery unfolds deeper mysteries still. Each insight whets our appetite for more.

Oh, yes! That's what all that "seeing through a glass darkly" stuff was about.

When people ask me biblical questions for which I don't know the answer or when I struggle to understand life's complications, like suffering and evil, I comfort myself with the idea that I'll "ask God when I get there" (that is, "there" to God—face to face).

The best mystery of all is that when I get *there*, I won't need to ask.

STORY (OF GOD)

It is fashionable these days to discuss the Bible and doctrine and the Church in terms of "story." Of course, it is true—Christianity depends on the combined stories of Israel and Jesus of Nazareth and certain claims about what those stories mean.

Corruptions arise, however, from several directions, depending upon our attitude about the reliability of the narrative and about its application beyond a limited number of people. Some folk like to dismiss the biblical story as merely fanciful imagination or as the exaggerated legends of a deluded people. Somehow there is a superciliousness about this stance that I find disgusting. What gives individuals the right to say—from the outside—that we who live inside a story don't know what we're talking about? What gives modern people the cockiness to think that they are remarkably smarter than communities from earlier eras? The harried craziness of contemporary life and its dependence on stock market reports, violent entertainments, massive accumulations of gadgets, and squandering of the earth does not convince me that folk in this era are so much wiser.

On the opposite side of the spectrum, God's story is corrupted by those who dogmatize it, become rigid about their dogma, mindlessly repeat the story without exploring it afresh, or turn the story and their understanding of it into insiders' jargon that doesn't communicate with the rest of the world. The result is a private story into which no one else is invited.

God's story is large and constantly widening. Above the desk at which I write hangs an exquisite painting done by

111

an artist in Kunming, China, and showing people from many regions of China and other parts of the world flooding down the hills in their traditional costumes, playing their musical instruments and dancing, and gathering around Jesus. The painting displays the glorious vision in Revelation 7:9–12 (cited in Chinese characters on its upper right corner) of a multitude drawn to worship Jesus from "every nation and all tribes and peoples and tongues."

This is the story we celebrate. We ruin it if we become too hardened by our own explanations of its meanings. John Yoder describes the Bible's purposes this way:

> It seems to be firm in this original testimony that the apostles were concerned to communicate a story and not a metaphysic. They were not argumentative about the ultimate nature of reality or about what set of words fit best to explain everything important. They were reporting something that had happened, something whose very quality as event had bowled them over and changed their lives, had surprised them. They were throwing themselves completely into the meaning of that event as its witnesses, and they were inviting their hearers to join as participants in the same story.[3]

The issue is not so much whether we can justify the story, but how it justifies us.

FORGIVENESS

For those of you who might be reading this book in order rather than choosing words at random it might seem strange to put forgiveness near the beginning of a section on actions of God. My decision to discuss it here was motivated by Miroslav Volf's recounting of an old Jewish story in which God, after deciding to create the world, "foresaw all the sin that human beings would commit against God and each other. The only way God could continue was to decide to forgive the world before creating it. Strange as it may seem, the commitment to forgive comes before creation."[4] Volf's emphasis on the precedence of forgiveness highlights one of the reasons that the Church confesses in the Nicene Creed that the Son was begotten of the Father before all worlds.[5]

The Jewish story helpfully counteracts our tendency to cheapen forgiveness by turning it into merely discounting, overlooking, dismissing, or utterly forgetting our sins and sinfulness. It reminds us of the grievousness of sins and suggests how much forgiveness loses its weight if we don't have a profound enough sense of our own sins and the entirety of human sin.

How readily we think that God's action of forgiveness is not difficult for the Trinity. After all, we are quite glib in our own dispensing of approval. It's so easy to be smug. Such excellent absolutions we administer and admire—and altogether ignore our own sins, shortcomings, downright failures, and blasphemings.

Throughout this whole section on the actions of God we must keep the immensity of sin in mind, for many of the works of God discussed herein were necessitated by our desperate condition and depraved capacity. All the movements of God below will display how incredibly much our forgiveness cost the Trinity.

Could we more thoroughly learn from God both the cost of forgiveness and the willingness to pay it? Surely we corrupt forgiveness by our inability to imitate it, as illustrated by the terribly apt (to us) parable of the unforgiving servant (Matt. 18:23–35). Only increased gratitude for God's forgiveness of us can instill the depth of love that will prevent our corruptions of forgiveness for others (Luke 7:36–50).

Perhaps we could frequently pray with Kierkegaard,

> Father in Heaven! Hold not up our sins against us, but hold us up against our sins, so that the thought of thee when it wakens in our soul—and each time it wakens—should not remind us of what we have committed but of what thou didst forgive; not of how we went astray but of how thou didst save us! Amen.[6]

CREATION

Why do we so often abuse the words *creation* or *creativity* by applying them to our petty imitations, our borrowed insights, our supposed brilliances, our paltry clevernesses? How much more honest it would be if we would acknowledge that we are but the vessels of a great Creator and highly privileged to participate in triune masterpieces. We haven't really originated those thoughts or works. As the Preacher reminds us, "There is nothing new under the sun." But oh! the rapture of discovering truths already there! And oh! the passion that flows in and through us when we stumble upon the part of divine creation that is ours to convey!

Or why do we sometimes hide the gifts of the Creator Spirit by wasting our lives in fervent, but frivolous, quests for our own achievements, for the fulfillment of our own ambitions— when God yearns to display immense originality through us if we could only learn dependence and trust? Why do we keep chasing after fame or distinction, after honors or belongings when the cosmos could be ours to admire and savor?

Surely our vauntings and ventings corrupt the creation as much as those who deny its Source altogether—though I can't for the life of me figure out how anybody could think that all the wonders which surround us could have developed by chance.

And indeed: I can't imagine it for the life of me.

When a measles virus killed my teenaged pancreas, so many other aspects of bodily health suffered too. The delicate intertwining of organs, flesh, hair, even the luster of eyes—the wonder of the body's cohesion became clear to me as I witnessed its breakdown.

Twenty years later, one eye hemorrhaging and two surgeries failing led me to marvel at the sagacity of two-eyed vision, and now I regularly laugh (or cry) at the ineptness of my pseudo-sight. Do you realize that one can't see a brown bird against a tree limb if one doesn't have depth perception?

I chuckle, too, if I discover a voice on my left that I thought was on my right because my partial deafness prohibits accurate locating. Do you ever thank the Creator for your built-in stereo soundings?

When I stumble—and fall now and then—because I don't feel my feet, I can't help but marvel at the creation of nerves and balance. Truly we wouldn't choose to have pain, but what a divinely inspired favor it is.[7]

And now, because I don't feel my feet, I've badly burned the crippled one and have struggled to live on crutches for the past two months (with more than one to go). Not only is everything SO M U C H S L O W E R because I can't just walk into a room and pick up what I need or run to the bookcase and grab a book I want for writing, but my other leg has become grotesquely swollen and unalterably painful because it has to bear the whole body's weight. Isn't it sensational (with all meanings intended) that the Creator designed us with *two* feet for locomotion and *two* hands for manipulation?

But enough of the negative. I constantly see the impossibility of an "accidental" or unmindful creation in the incredible moments when the body works. When I had cancer and the chemotherapy left me wretchedly listless and lifeless, what a difference it made when an injected hormone punched my bone marrow into producing red cells! That hormone, natural to most folk, still keeps my energy (and spirits) up. Isn't it phenomenal that our red blood cells distribute energy opulently throughout our systems?

And now, as I watch the progressive healing of my burned foot, I am dazzled by the curative properties of blood and skin. How does a wound know that it must begin healing at the innermost slash and work outward, so that the greenly-dead cells get pushed up and out? How do the vessels know that they should bring lots of blood and join the fray with white-celled ferocity against the invader germs? How does the body heal itself? (Of course, it doesn't! The triune persons recreate us through their own clever devices of Word and Breath!)

And how many more monumental facets of our bodily frame and mental acuities and sensate faculties and soul-full personalities could we name (if we just tried) that display the glories of our Maker's matchless originality? Maybe if we stopped more often to contemplate our internal marvels, we'd transcend our selves in trusting their Source to work through us in true creativity.

CREATION II

Why *do* the particles arrange themselves

every
morning

in b
a
n
d
s

d across the sky
of   r
a
colors   w
p
that spread from the horizon u

GLOWING!

How *do* the particles know?

First one thin strip of pink to catch an eye,

then a larger puff of pillows blushing to be awakened,

and suddenly the largest mass of clouds explodes

beyond the window's

frame

in multi-hued billows of rose,

to brighten soon

to paler white, but

luminous

s.
t
f
a
h
s

Where did the particles learn to paint?

118

CREATION III

Two entries on creation aren't enough. It is so irksome that even in churches God's colossal creation is diminished by applying the name *Creator* as if it designated only the first member of the Trinity. To reduce God to functions—and only one duty for each person at that—is to lose the splendor of the Word spangling the heavens with galaxies and the tumult of the Spirit's whirlwind as the divine Breath heaves tectonic plates and black holes and gravitational powers throughout the cosmos.

Someone gave me a magnificently mind-boggling, unbelievably beautiful, absolutely astounding book of photographs, taken by the Hubble telescope, of the enormous proportions and intricate complexities of space spectacles. Those of us who are not scientists can only gawk and gape, but even those who understand (somewhat) these cosmic configurations find that their explanations lead them to a Mind larger than their own.

Sharon Begley, senior editor at *Newsweek*, comments in her Introductory Essay to that book, *The Hand of God*, "ironically, the more focused the portraits from deep space, the more meticulous and specific our calculations, the more it seems improbable, even impossible, that our world could have been an arbitrary occurrence."[8]

Besides the immensity of the creation, we dare never lose sight of God's celestial Joy in doing it. C. S. Lewis imagines Aslan creating Narnia by singing and puts into a child's mind our wonder at the mystery:

All this time the Lion's song, and his stately prowl, to and fro, backward and forward, was going on. . . . Polly was finding the song more and more interesting because she thought she was beginning to see the connection between the music and the things that were happening. When a line of dark firs sprang up on a ridge about a hundred yards away she felt that they were connected with a series of deep, prolonged notes which the Lion had sung a second before. And when he burst into a rapid series of lighter notes she was not surprised to see primroses suddenly appearing in every direction. Thus, with an unspeakable thrill, she felt quite certain that all the things were coming (as she said) "out of the Lion's head." When you listened to his song you heard the things he was making up: when you looked round you, you saw them. This was so exciting that she had no time to be afraid.[9]

Oh, the splendor and the beauty and the immensity and the distinctiveness of God's creations! Oh, the fragility and the potency and the simplicity and the intricacy of God's designs! Oh, the purpose and the ingenuity and the profundity and the vitality of God's patterns!

Perhaps the poet of the apocryphal Ecclesiasticus said it best:

> What a masterpiece is the clear vault of the sky!
> How glorious is the spectacle of the heavens!
> The sun comes into view proclaiming as it rises
> how marvellous a thing it is, made by the Most High.
> At noon it parches the earth,
> and no one can endure its blazing heat.
> The stoker of a furnace works in the heat,
> but three times as hot is the sun scorching the hills.
> It breathes out fiery vapours,
> and its glare blinds the eyes.
> Great is the Lord who made it,
> whose word speeds it on its course.
>
> He made the moon also to serve in its turn,
> a perpetual sign to mark the divisions of time.
> From the moon, feast-days are reckoned;
> it is a light that wanes as it completes its course.

120

The moon gives its name to the month;
it waxes marvellously as its phases change,
a beacon to the armies of heaven,
shining in the vault of the sky.

The brilliant stars are the beauty of the sky,
a glittering array in the heights of the Lord.
At the commands of the Holy One they stand in their
appointed place;
they never default at their post.

Look at the rainbow and praise its Maker;
it shines with a supreme beauty,
rounding the sky with its gleaming arc,
a bow bent by the hands of the Most High.

His command speeds the snow-storm
and sends the swift lightning to execute His sentence.
To that end the storehouses are opened,
and the clouds fly out like birds.
By His mighty power the clouds are piled up
and the hailstones broken small.
The crash of His thunder makes the earth writhe,
and, when He appears, an earthquake shakes the hills.
At His will the south wind blows,
the squall from the north and the hurricane.
He scatters the snow-flakes like birds alighting;
they settle like a swarm of locusts.
The eyes is dazzled by their beautiful whiteness,
and as they fall the mind is entranced. . . .

By the power of His thought He tamed the deep
and planted it with islands.
Those who sail the sea tell stories of its dangers,
which astonish all who hear them;
in it are strange and wonderful creatures,
all kinds of living things and huge sea-monsters.
By His own action He achieves His end,
and by His word all things are held together.

However much we say, we cannot exhaust our theme;
to put it in a word: He is all.

Where can we find the skill to sing His praises?
For He is greater than all His works.
The Lord is terrible and very great,
and marvellous is His power.
Honour the Lord to the best of your ability,
and He will still be high above all praise.
Summon all your strength to declare His greatness,
and be untiring, for the most you can do will fall short.
Has anyone ever seen Him, to be able to describe Him?
Can anyone praise Him as He truly is?
We have seen but a small part of His works,
and there remain many mysteries greater still.

Ecclesiasticus 43:1–18, 25–32 (NEB)

THE OLD TESTAMENT

The "Old Testament" or "Hebrew Scriptures" testimony to God's dealings with the people Israel (and others) is corrupted most often by being ignored, as if Christians could live without our roots! Equally foolish is to think that the Old Testament has been superseded by the New so that none of it applies to us now (or that the Jewish people have been replaced by the Church as God's Chosen People). To our shame, the name *Old* contributes to these horrible misconceptions, since in our era that word is usually associated with things that are old-fashioned, outdated, worn out, no longer sufficiently fast or functional in light of what is new.

I try to avoid both of the above corruptions by calling the larger part of the biblical testimony the "First" Testament. That name emphasizes that we need it, that it is fundamental to the Second Testament, that it is of prime significance. It also helps offset the mistaken notion that God is different in the two segments.

As children some of us were taught, "the Old Testament is Law and the New Testament is Gospel," or somewhere we acquired the idea that God is full of wrath in the Old Testament and thoroughly loving in the New. Such heresies ought to be squelched once and for all.

After excellent teachers dispensed with the divided-Bible misunderstanding, it didn't take me long to learn to love the Old/First Testament. I love how God sets me free from the very beginning as a woman bearing the divine image, called to be a "helper corresponding," entrusted with the care of the earth, reminded that the Creator has provided food enough for all—and all that in just Genesis 1 and 2!

123

I love how God calls a people and blesses them to be a blessing, rescues them from their oppressors—and, more important, from themselves—forms them throughout their history to move away from the violence of the nations that surrounded them,[10] promises to be their God, and fulfills all the covenantal promises even though Israel continually broke their own.

Of course, there isn't room in this book even to start exploring all the stimulating genres in the Hebrew people's treasury, but I do wish I could at least begin to spur some Christians' delight in it and faithfulness to it.

WRATH

At a few clergy conferences I have heard other speakers say that we ought to dispense with the wrath of God—as if we human beings have the right to discard parts of the Bible according to our own preferences. Of course, we all want God to be loving and kind. The wrath of God is too terrible and too mysterious for us, so we'd rather just ignore it.

On the other side of the theological spectrum, some people like to emphasize the wrath of God. Eternal fire and brimstone, they think, should be threatened regularly—as if scaring the hell out of people will make good disciples out of them.

What is missing in both of these opposite corruptions is serious reading of the texts. If we look carefully at the (primarily First Testament) stories that illustrate God's wrath, we will notice that God never wants to vent wrath, but must because of the destructiveness of our rebellions and wickednesses, that the LORD's wrath is never contaminated with sin, that instead the Covenant Keeper's anger is coupled with profound grief and divinely unbroken promises. Most important, triune love always undergirds God's efforts to win back His heinously defiant and faithlessly unrepentant people and to prevent devastating effects of human sin on the entire cosmos. Throughout the Bible God is ready to turn away from wrath if people turn away from their evil; moreover, God takes evil into the divine self rather than letting it wreak destruction. Always God's wrath is part of the Trinity's purposes of rescue.[11]

The reason that I want to reclaim the wrath of God is that without it we don't properly handle the injustices and cruelties of our world. Only within the framework of divine anger against all that violates God's creative, saving, and sustaining purposes will we be righteously angry about ethnic cleansing and religious persecution, oppressive labor practices, the global AIDs crisis, famines and poverty and malnutrition, wars, corporate graft and greed, and every other form of evil which kills or reduces people. Only when we let the vengeance be God's can we fight these evils righteously. Only when we remember God's final wrathful restoration of the cosmos do we have courage to counteract the extensive ecological destruction of our times. Only when we notice God's tears do we learn that wrath is a subset of love more than of holiness.

COMMANDMENTS

Why is it that we are so good at reducing God's commandments? Why, for example, do we think the divine commandment to keep the Sabbath day holy means only that we should show up at a church building for an hour or so once a month (!) or so? Or why do we think that "thou shalt not kill" does not apply to abortion or to war? Why do we laugh at television or movie covetings or accept it when politicians steal other politicians' reputations? We are experts at trivializing God's mandates, as if that could make us any less of sinners.

On the other hand, sometimes we corrupt God's commandments by turning them into rules by which we can judge others and accuse them of greater sins than our own. We are experts at speck hunting and plank dismissing.

All of these expertises derive from our corrupting of God's commanding. We forget that commanding is a component of creating, that direction comes as an element of sustaining. It might be compared to the gift of the instruction book that accompanies a technological device. Since the company that produced the gadget knows how it works, we are quite silly if we don't follow its instruction book. If we don't, we might wind up with ink or oil on our hands or with jammed paper or a malfunctioning toy.

Don't we realize how much God's commandments are good for us? If only we could recover from our Jewish forebears their love for God's *Torah* or instruction. It was not God's commands against which the apostle Paul railed in the New Testament—for how else could the Psalmist say such things as "I find my delight in your commandments, because I love them" (Ps. 119:47)? Rather, both Jesus and Paul opposed

127

those who corrupt the *Torah* in ways described above and forget that God's "decrees are righteous forever." Could we learn again to plead, "give me understanding that I may live" (Ps. 119:144)? Indeed, the whole First Testament is filled with narratives that show the benefits to those who love and obey God's commands and the disorders that befall the disobedient because of their own choice for death rather than life (see Deuteronomy 30).

Could we learn again how good for us God's commanding is? Wouldn't it be wonderful if we never had to lock our cars or houses because nobody ever burglarized? So isn't it a great gift that God commands us not to steal?

Wouldn't we be glad if we never had to worry about terrorist strikes or random gunfire, about abortions or any wars, about injurious words or malevolent actions, because no one ever destroyed human life? So isn't it a grace that God commands us not to kill?

Wouldn't our bodies, souls, social relationships, and spirits be healthier if we engaged in sexual union only within the framework of a covenantal, faithful marriage? Why do we believe our society's lies about the "meaningfulness" of "sex" outside the boundaries of God's genuinely loving ordering?

Has anyone who coveted ever been truly happy? Don't we see the danger (to ourselves as well as to a sustainable earth) of a society whose entire economy is based on the continuous stirring up of discontent?

Won't we ever learn that worshiping anything or anyone else besides God is to violate the precise nature of our self, created in God's image to praise Him ceaselessly? How could we ever be happy being other than we were made to be? Why do we keep choosing death instead?

THE VIRGINAL CONCEPTION

For most of my life I have corrupted the name for this action of God by calling it "the virgin birth"—which certainly did not occur. All the biblical testimonies suggest that Jesus' birth took place in the usual way—except that it transpired in an unusual place and amid not the best of circumstances. But a "virginal conception"—that is an entirely different matter.

The doctrine of the "virginal conception" is corrupted whenever people think that it can either prove or disprove Jesus' deity. Actually, a virginal conception would not have been necessary to "make Jesus God," and, on the other hand, some religious myths produce all sorts of gods without any miraculous reproductions.

Mennonite theologian John Yoder lays out the deepest corruption of this doctrine by reminding us, first, that the core controversy is a question of history. What really happened? If that is the issue, then "answers from grounds other than history are inappropriate."

Often the traditional doctrine is denied on foundations such as "the modern philosophical commitment of the scientific worldview that says things like the [virginal conception] do not happen and therefore it could not have happened." This, Yoder charges, is not a historical statement. It is not derived from returning to Jesus' time and examining what actually occurred on the basis of the only sources we have—namely, the witnesses. "It is a philosophical denial and as such is illegitimate. Philosophical grounds may raise a question. They may make belief difficult. But the belief is no more difficult than the philosophical assumptions themselves are questionable."

129

Lest those who accept the doctrine of the virginal conception overplay their defense, we must also here repudiate philosophical grounds as the rationale for that affirmation. Yoder comments that "some of the conservative defensiveness on the point has also been philosophical; that is, it argues about the logic of things rather than about the witnesses."[12] He emphasizes,

> How we take the reports of the [virginal conception] is not really a test of biblical authority. It is not a test of whether we believe the Bible. It is rather a test of hermeneutics—how we understand the Bible. The question is not whether Matthew and Luke say that Jesus was born of a virgin. We know that. The question is what they mean by it. (168–169)

That is why the question of the virginal conception is an important one to raise here, for most of the words and phrases considered in this book ultimately depend upon how we understand the Bible. Can we trust the witnesses?

Ultimately, "It is not possible to answer a historical question with *absolute* certainty, but only with *historical* certainty" (170, emphasis mine). That is why our position on biblical authority, whatever it is, is not a legitimate basis for a decision about this historical question.

There are two things, Yoder concludes, we can say about the issue historically—"[f]irst, that the only sources we have on the virgin[al conception] affirm it, and second that we cannot think of any especially plausible reason that anyone would have had to invent it, since it is not a very helpful idea in the ancient near Eastern world" (171).

Yoder's comments provide wise guidance for thinking about many of the words I ache to reclaim in this book. What do the Bible's authors say? Did they have anything to gain—besides rejection and possibly death—by saying what they did? Why would they give this testimony if they were not convinced it were true? They don't give any evidence of being seriously deceived, nor are their testimonies limited to the cosmologies of their time. As Jacques Ellul said, "it was not easier for the contemporaries of Isaiah or of Jesus to understand what they were saying than for our contemporaries"[13]; this is also true for the biblical writers. Some might think that this is a way to cop out of the enormous issues involved in such debates. But Yoder summarizes that, instead, this is "our first duty . . . to deal with a narrative text as historians by testing whether the witnesses are credible and otherwise leaving it at that" (172).[14]

Many of us who test the witnesses find them credible and continue to name God in ways they have taught us. We believe that the Holy Spirit came upon Mary and that the power of God accomplished in that virgin a miraculous conception. It is too beautiful not to be believed. And, as Martin Luther said, "it is no less a miracle that [Mary] refrained from pride and arrogance than that she received the gifts she did."[15] It is no less an attested miracle than Jesus' resurrection or than God's "new creation" in Christ Jesus of all of us.

THE INCARNATION

It seems odd to me that many who stress that Jesus calls Christians to "incarnate" the Gospel in present times (that is, those who advocate something of a social gospel) and thereby concentrate on the humanity of Jesus and His life in the midst of the world's nitty-gritty, meanwhile actually are the very ones who deny that *God* was in Christ incarnated in the physical body of Jesus of Nazareth. They often also reject Jesus' bodilyness in His resurrection and the hope that we, too, will someday physically rise from the dead to enjoy eternal life in an incorruptible bodily form of some sort.

This rejection of divine incarnation is dangerous because it urges us to invest ourselves in a hopeless cause. Works that attempt to "incarnate" Christ's life in this world are indeed good, but we must admit both that no human but Jesus is "God incarnate" and that our deeds are insufficient to change the world. The only thing that will recreate everything anew is the culmination of God's purposes in the new heaven and new earth. At that time, too, we will enjoy the fullness of life eternal, incorruptible—totally by God's grace brought to us by God's incarnation in Jesus Christ!

On the other side of the theological spectrum—and equally odd—those who insist the most on the physicality of Jesus' resurrection and ours often do not actively engage in works of peacemaking and justice building for the sake of meeting the physical needs of our neighbors in this world. While the opposite theological pole rejects the culmination of the incarnation, this side rejects its "meanwhile."

How much fleshly-ness, embodiment can we stand in Jesus? in God? in ourselves?

Ultimately we're asking whether Jesus as human could really be the fullness of deity. Could God take flesh and die?[16] And we have to ask, then, what are the implications for my enfleshed existence? Can our fullness of humanity be also a place where God dwells now?

St. Athanasius (298–373) long ago realized that there was an even deeper truth beneath the particular incarnation in Jesus of Nazareth—that God is cosmically incarnated:

> For this purpose, then ["to recreate all . . . to suffer on behalf of all and to be an ambassador for all with the Father"] the incorporeal and incorruptible and immaterial Word of God entered our world. In one sense, indeed, He was not far from it before, for no part of creation had ever been without Him Who, while ever abiding in union with the Father, yet fills all things that are. But now He entered the world in a new way, stooping to our level in His love and Self-revealing to us.[17]

Athanasius exults that the incarnate Jesus "banished death from us and made us anew; and, invisible and imperceptible as in Himself He is, He became visible through His works and revealed Himself as the Word of the Father, the Ruler and King of the whole creation" (27).

One of the most important gifts of the incarnation for me is that God in Jesus thereby demonstrates the lengths to which the Trinity would go to bring me back to Himself.

We too easily forget that our body is our self in union with all the rest of each of us. The ancient Hebrew literature thought more appropriately about the unity of body, soul, spirit, mind, and kidneys (their term for what we designate by the metaphorical word *heart*). All of these are included in the wholeness of life. I rejoice, then, that Jesus came to the earth as God in bodily form; that He invested His whole self—body, soul, spirit, mind, and bowels (the Greek choice for the source of emotions)—in the lives of the people He encountered; that He gave over His body into human death; that He rose triumphant over bodily death; that He remains and reigns as our ascended, incarnate Lord. As 1 Timothy 3:16 declares,

Without any doubt, the mystery of our religion is great:
    He was revealed in flesh,
        vindicated in spirit,
            seen by angels,
        proclaimed among Gentiles,
            believed in throughout the world,
                taken up in glory.

That God/Man embodiment frees me to put my body at the service of others—to invest in them with everything I am and all my energy and strength. That Jesus was truly man gives me courage to be tired in kingdom work, to suffer for righteousness' sake, even to die. That Jesus was truly God promises me that He truly lives in me by the power of the Holy Spirit to incarnate the Gospel afresh—and never in vain, for God *will* accomplish the cosmic purposes in which we are privileged to participate. The Trinity has surely invested in us to the hilt.

Two Natures (of Christ)

Do we really appreciate the immensity of this truth that Jesus was both true God and true man in order to accomplish the triune work of rescuing us from ourselves and redoing all of creation? Many question it, or overemphasize one side or the other of the dialectic of God and man, but certainly none of us can comprehend its astonishing implications for our relationship with God and for the way we live.

For example, I corrupt this doctrine every time I complain about how tough my life is or think it is unfair to have to go through various afflictions or to endure certain troubles. Dorothy Sayers, in her typical forthright wit, chides me with this reminder:

> Jesus . . . was in fact and in truth, and in the most exact and literal sense of the words, "the God by whom all things were made." . . . He was not merely a man so good as to be "like God"—He was God . . . for whatever reason God chose to make man as he is—limited and suffering and subject to sorrows and death—He had the honesty and the courage to take His own medicine. Whatever game He is playing with His creation, He has kept His own rules and played fair. He can exact nothing from man that He has not exacted from Himself. He has Himself gone through the whole of human experience, from the trivial irritations of family life and the cramping restrictions of hard work and lack of money to the worst horrors of pain and humiliation, defeat, despair, and death. When He was a man, He played the man. He was born in poverty and died in disgrace, and thought it well worthwhile.[18]

Who are we to complain about our lives when God took His own medicine?

Lest we leave it at that and forget the other side of the dialectic—that this humanness of God was for reasons of the Trinity's extraordinary purposes on our behalf—we need constant reminders of the double emphases (and their constant tension) in the New Testament. Alan Lewis goes so far as to say, "the double origination of Jesus, with God and in a human family, betrays the opposition of incompatible Christologies within the New Testament." Those Christologies, or interpretations of Christ's person and work, are indeed incompatible, but both true—and it is in our failure to hang on to them both equally tenaciously that we corrupt His name and His action of coming to earth on our behalf.

Remarkably freshly and appropriately, Lewis emphasizes both sides of the biblical picture. First, "no less than Mark and John, the same evangelists who record this miraculous conception [Matthew and Luke] also portray Jesus as thoroughly—and scandalously—ordinary." On the other side,

> At most (*though it could mean everything*), they convey an intuition that the very possibility and actuality of Christ's existence, in the fullness of his humanness, was no contingent accident of history, but the specific gift of God's grace and the accomplishment of divine initiative and power.[19]

Lewis helps us realize that we, along with the biblical writers, only begin to glimpse all that it means for God to have become human in Christ. Could we ever get done praising the Trinity for the indescribable gift of the God-in-man Christ? Could we ever quit yearning to comprehend it more thoroughly? Imagine if the Shoemaker would become a shoe!

MIRACLES

Why do people like to think in our modern scientific culture that Jesus couldn't have done the miracles recorded in the Bible? Objectors don't believe God would intervene in the world in such a way—or they assume that the writers of the Bible were silly, premodern people who too gullibly believed supernatural explanations for phenomena that could be naturally explained once the world gained enough technical expertise.[20]

But how cramped it makes our lives not to believe in miracles. We miss the wonder of every day. It is indeed astonishing that chubby bumblebees can fly or that hummingbirds can keep up their tremendous pace of flapping.

By the usual dictionary definition—that a miracle is something that seems to contradict natural laws and therefore is thought to be due to supernatural causes—I've experienced miracles. All the doctors and nurses attending me in a California hospital were amazed at the speed of my recuperation from a bowel resectioning necessitated when 15" of me became gangrenous after my bowel intussuscepted (or strangled itself). Even more miraculous to my mind was that the attending doctor just couldn't rest when he didn't find an explanation for how sick I was and, consequently, he called for surgery at 10 p.m. If he hadn't operated, the intussusception (rarely seen in adults) would probably have been fatal. God will heal us all perfectly at the last day; why should we doubt that God might occasionally give us a foretaste of that in a "miraculous" healing?

We hear stories of miracles frequently.[21] Why should we doubt them? A Notre Dame law school graduate, whose mother died on his first birthday, knew only his stepmother as mother since people didn't talk about death in those days. In the first grade he had surgery and during the night hemorrhaged severely while he was sleeping. Meanwhile, he dreamed that a beautiful woman with dark skin and long black hair came to him, touched his shoulder, and softly repeated, "Tommy, wake up." Aroused, he found himself lying in a pool of blood and called his dad, who applied pressure and rushed him to the hospital where the emergency room doctor observed that another 15 minutes of bleeding would have been fatal. A few months later, in response to his questions, he learned of his birth mother and was shown her picture, "the same lady who woke me up in my dream."[22]

I was spiritually strengthened by Tom's story and moved to gratitude—but I know people who react only by asking why such things only happen to a few. It seems, though, that we are so desensitized by the glitz and fantasy of contemporary media that we usually fail to recognize the constant occurrence *in every life* of all sorts of things remarkable, surprising, wonder-full.

On the opposite side of the miracle doubters or mockers are the miracle demanders, those who think they have the right to require them from God or to expect a certain kind of healing miracle. Such persons often limit the sorts of healing that God should do and criticize those of us who don't experience physical improvement (I've had plenty of these ordeals, too) as if it were our fault for not "praying right." Don't they realize that the miracle might be one of attitudinal change or an increase in trust or dependence instead of a physical benefit?

To corrupt miracles by demanding them or insisting on a certain kind is to drown gratitude in arrogance and selfishness and to miss the true gifts of God because we want something less. I am more guilty of this category of corruption because I get so impatient with infirmities and lose sight of the greater miracles God wants to do in my character or ministry or who knows what else.

Tom Wright exposes all our truncations of miracles when he says, "In any case, I think God can do whatever God wants.

I don't think we know what the limits are. And our discussion of the limits is too much shaped by the terms of modern philosophy."[23]

That everything good is a miracle is illustrated well by the joke about scientists who claimed they could produce human life, so they undertook a competition with God. God took the dust of the earth and formed a man and breathed into him the breath of life. The scientists in their turn picked up some soil and began to work, but God immediately stopped them by saying, "No. You have to come up with your own dirt."

God always makes bread for the billions by multiplying the wonder-full potential of seeds, planted in productive soil and nourished by divine gifts of sunshine and rain. Why couldn't Jesus simply speed up the process and quickly multiply bread for a few thousand?

TEACHING

It has been popular for the last two centuries to reduce Jesus by naming Him simply as a great moral teacher—or a wandering prophet, cynic, peasant philosopher, or whatever other names contemporary theologians like to use. Long ago, C. S. Lewis responded to this corruption in his famous verdict that either Jesus was who He said He was—Savior of the cosmos, Ruler over the kingdom of God, Resurrection and Life, and so forth—or else He couldn't be a good teacher because He was either lying (so why would we trust His teaching?) or a lunatic (somewhat on the order of a person who called himself a poached egg). Lewis made it clear that we all must make a choice. Either Jesus was and is truly the Son of God, or else He was deranged or something worse. We can admit Him to an institution for the insane, we can torture Him and crucify Him as a criminal, or we can worship Him as our Lord and God. But we cannot simply patronize Him as if He were merely a great moral teacher because He did not, and did not intend to, give us that option.[24]

The same kind of patronizing nonsense against which Lewis protested still persists in our times, but I'm also concerned about a different sort of corruption of Jesus' teachings—the outrage that many who call Jesus "Lord and God" don't want to take seriously what He taught about the kingdom.

Jesus, our Lord and God, made it clear that in His coming the kingdom of God was brought to the world (see especially Mark 1:14–15, where the perfect verb tense underscores the kingdom's initiation in Jesus and its continuation now that

He's here). That the kingdom of God is the most essential aspect of Jesus' teachings is underscored by the fact that in His last days with His disciples, the forty days between His resurrection and ascension, Jesus focused His teaching on issues of the kingdom (Acts 1:3; see also Luke 8:1 and the many texts in which He sends out the disciples). If we call Jesus our King, then why don't we live according to the way of His kingdom? Consider some of His descriptions of kingdom life.

For example, Jesus said the kingdom grows like seed—we know not how (Mark 4:26–29). Then why do churches plan strategies by which they can "grow" their numbers? Or why do congregations set target goals for how many people will be "converted" in a certain number of years? Isn't the growth up to God and not to us?

Jesus said that the kingdom of God belongs to children and that none of us can enter it unless we become like children (Mark 10:14–15; Luke 18:16–17). Then why do our churches so often send the children away during worship? Do we not have much to learn from them about receiving the kingdom? And why do we keep them away from the community that claims to be worshiping Jesus?

Jesus said that it was hard for the wealthy to enter the kingdom of God (Mark 10:23), that instead it was the poor and persecuted to whom the kingdom belongs (Luke 6:20; Matt. 5:3, 10). Then why are our North American churches so rich? Why do we find it so hard to share our wealth with the rest of the world? After all, Jesus said the kingdom is so precious that we would sell our all to possess it (Matt. 13:44) and that because a rich person has too much he lacks the greatest treasure of all (Mark 10:17–22). If we call Jesus our King, could we not learn to seek His kingdom first and trust that everything else will then be added (Matt. 6:33)?

In the face of the immense sexual idolatry of our culture, ought we not to take Jesus more seriously when He tells us that refraining from sexual involvement is a choice one could make for the sake of the kingdom (Matt. 19:12)?

Perhaps most important these days, Jesus said that in His kingdom His people should love their enemies (Matt. 5:38–48).

Then how could anyone who claims to be a Christian, a citizen of the kingdom, support a nation that chooses pre-emptively to attack its enemies?

How can we call Jesus our Lord and not follow His teaching? Isn't that simply to call our Teacher a lunatic?

SUFFERING

For centuries of Church history leaders thought that God was impassible—that is, that the divine could not suffer. In the debates connected with the Church councils held at Nicaea and Constantinople, at which the doctrines of the Trinity and of the two natures of Christ were discussed, for some people a distinction between Christ's human nature and His divinity became such a separation that only the human Jesus suffered. The axiom of impassibility was too strong for those people to imagine that God Himself actually suffered in Christ. Indeed, it is the scandal of the cross that God Himself suffered and died![25]

It is a great gift to Christian faith that in recent decades theologians have been reclaiming the biblical texts that narrate *God's* suffering throughout the history of His people and thereby help us all to take more seriously the particular, historical sufferings of the God-Man Jesus.[26] Even with the rejection of the doctrine of God's impassibility and with the recovery of a doctrine of God's suffering, we still must deal with contemporary corruptions.

One corruption is actually fostered by the Christian creeds in their English versions, which seem to limit Jesus' sufferings to His last few days. The most common English version of the Apostle's Creed says,

> He suffered under Pontius Pilate,
> was crucified, died, and was buried.

Let's change one comma to make the sentence more accurate and confess instead,

He suffered,
under Pontius Pilate was crucified, died, and was buried.

Similarly, in newer versions of the Nicene Creed, we recite,

For our sake he was crucified under Pontius Pilate;
he suffered death and was buried,

which suggest that Jesus suffered only in death. Older versions of that creed instead proclaimed that "he suffered and was buried."

These are not trivial quibblings, for Jesus did not suffer only under Pontius Pilate or merely when He died. Jesus' birth involved the sufferings of poverty, of scandal, of a smelly manger and scratchy hay. Jesus suffered as a refugee from Herod, as a teacher misunderstood by both His family and His closest disciples, as a homeless travelling rabbi constantly worn out by pushy crowds and harassing religious leaders.

Not only did Jesus suffer more in His entire life than we usually acknowledge, but also His sufferings in His last days were more extreme than we customarily imagine. I don't mean merely that we should focus more on the brutality of His physical punishment as Mel Gibson did in his controversial movie about the Passion. Certainly many people who have been political prisoners have been tortured far more extensively, for much longer periods of time.

I intend instead for us not to undervalue the cost of Christ's obedience, the severity of the rupture within God's self in the God-forsakenness of Christ's total submission to all the powers of evil and His descent to hell. As Alan Lewis makes clear, too often Christians jump too easily to Easter and don't spend enough time in Holy Saturday looking back to Good Friday without the hope of resurrection.[27]

I suppose we don't want to take Jesus' sufferings more seriously because we are not willing to bear them also. We'd rather not think that affliction and weakness are the way God usually works because we would prefer to be successful and powerful ourselves when we do God's work. Or we don't want to recognize that where Jesus is suffering today is in the lives of women, children, minorities, the poor, and others who are the victims of our sins.[28] I have been thinking about this quite a bit this Lent as I write. At various conferences people have said such things as "I gave up eating desserts for Lent," and I have found myself joking, "I gave up walking for Lent." But to me it is no laughing matter. I'm tired of the pain, of the swollenness of my other leg that's bearing my weight on crutches, of the preposterously long time it is taking for the burn on my foot to heal. For the past two months I have wished that looking at all the sufferings of Jesus would make me more willing to bear this comparatively minor inconvenience—but I don't seem to have become more willing, even though I know how small my trials are compared to those of so many in the world who suffer so deeply. I pray that someday I will trust God in everything.

I have become more grateful, I think, for all that Christ has done for me. I experienced a similar, but more dramatic surge of gratitude when I read this scene in G. K. Chesterton's wildly comic mystery, *The Man Who Was Thursday*, in which the devil shouts,

> "You are the seven angels of heaven, and you have had no troubles. Oh, I could forgive you everything, you that rule all mankind, if I could feel for once that you had suffered for one hour a real agony such as I—"

In response, Thursday, one of the main characters in the story, sprang to his feet and, trembling, cried,

> . . . "It is not true that we have never been broken. We have been broken upon the wheel. . . . We were complaining of unforgettable miseries even at the very moment when this man entered insolently to accuse us of happiness. I repel the slander; we have not been happy."

After a few more sentences he turned to see the strangely smiling face of the enigmatic Sunday, whose identity is at last revealed in this scene:

> "Have you," [Thursday] cried in a dreadful voice, "have you ever suffered?"

As he gazed, the great face grew to an awful size . . . It grew larger and larger, filling the whole sky; then everything went black. Only in the blackness before it entirely destroyed his brain he seemed to hear a distant voice saying a commonplace text that he had heard somewhere, "Can ye drink of the cup that I drink of?"[29]

CRUCIFIXION

There are all sorts of ways in which the crucifixion of Jesus has been corrupted throughout history—perhaps none so vile as that it is turned into a basis for anti-Semitism.[30] The Gospel writers certainly show the antipathy of certain Jewish leaders against Jesus, but His death, all of the New Testament makes clear, was caused by all of us—every human being throughout time and space.

Another way in which the crucifixion is distorted is illustrated by Mel Gibson's movie, *The Passion of Christ*, which seems to specialize in gore. The movie seems to say that Christ's crucifixion dealt with our human suffering because He bore more of it than anyone else, but as numerous commentators have pointed out—in secular as well as religious journals—that is not how the Scriptures have understood the meaning of the crucifixion.[31] Jesus' death was brutal, yes. Its salvific power, however, lies in *many* other factors—perhaps most thoroughly in His willingness to make the exchange of His totally innocent righteousness for our hopeless degradation.

A third kind of corruption has arisen because of the powerfully insightful works of René Girard, whose theory of scapegoating has been thought by many scholars to explain sufficiently the meaning of the crucifixion.[32] Girard's work is especially helpful, and Jesus' crucifixion does indeed serve as the fulfillment of the First Testament imagery and practice of sending the scapegoat away into the desert and certain death, but that is only one of the numerous biblical typologies which deepen the meaning of Christ's crucifixion.

Another means for deforming the crucifixion arises from those who limit the work of salvation to that event alone. This theological misunderstanding is heightened by jargonistic expressions related to the word *blood*. To say, for example, that "my sins are washed away in the blood of the cross" is not false, but it certainly isn't the whole truth. The crucifixion was somewhat of a culmination of Christ's entire work of redemption, but definitely not all that was necessary. It is but one piece of the entire fabric of Jesus' incarnation, life, teaching, sufferings, death, time in the grave, resurrection, and ascension.

On the opposite side of the theological spectrum of those who put all meaning into "the blood of the cross" are those who put no theological emphasis there. These are the scholars who insist that Jesus' death was simply the result of His teaching (problematic to religious leaders) and was without salvific intent or substitutionary effects. This corruption finds its epitome in those scholars who insist that Jesus' execution didn't "save" anybody.[33] To make light of God's purposes, suggested throughout the history of Israel, seems to me to be the most arrogant corruption of all. Who are we to say that the biblical writers are deluded when they testify that Jesus went to His death as our substitute and as a fulfillment of God's purposes since the beginning of time?

This corruption is augmented by the idea that Jesus was totally passive in the crucifixion. True, He did nothing to stop it. But all the Gospels show that Christ willingly chose to go through with it. He accepted this cup, this baptism, this sacrifice, this submission to the triune will. His death was not salvific because it was heroic—as movies tend to portray it—but because it was a "revolutionary subordination," which through its weakness and humility and obedience thereby triumphed over all the powers of evil[34] and completed the work of the promises to Israel.

All of the corruptions above arise because of failures of one sort or another to take the entire biblical record seriously. There are so many biblical types, images, symbols, metaphors, and theological elucidations scattered throughout both Testaments that to confine our understanding of the crucifixion to just one or two is to reduce a monumental mystery to banal buzz words.

We should learn instead from those who put together the Christian canon (who knew that we needed all the Hebrew Scriptures and four Gospel accounts, as well as the theological formulations of the epistles and the visionary symbols of The Revelation); from the Patristic saints, the mystics, the reformers, and theologians throughout the ages who ruminated on, and wrestled with, the meaning of the crucifixion; and most especially from the artists whose insights are displayed in clay and wood, paint and glass, musical instruments and voices that the crucifixion is a hideous and many-splendored thing, embedded in a capacious eternity of significances. Lent is a good time to expand our understanding by engaging in disciplines such as reading slowly through the Passion accounts in the four Gospels,[35] meditating on a good theologian/preacher's Holy Week sermons,[36] or listening to Johann Sebastian Bach's *St. Matthew Passion*.[37]

We must hear the frightful sounds of crucifixion, see its ugly violence, taste its hope in bread and wine, and touch its unfathomed intimacy. Perhaps none has said it better than Isaac Watts, who surveyed the wondrous cross in 1707 and concluded that the only fitting response was humility, repentance, sacrifice, wonder, and praise.

> See, from His head, His hands, His feet
> Sorrow and love flow mingled down;
> Did e'er such love and sorrow meet,
> Or thorns compose so rich a crown?
> Were the whole realm of nature mine,
> That were a tribute far too small;
> Love so amazing, so divine
> Demands my soul, my life, my all.

Indeed! The Christ of the crucifixion *shall have* my soul, my life, my all!

TEMPTATIONS

Can we actually imagine that the temptations of Jesus were real? Can we really understand that God could be tempted to be not God?

Sometimes I think we corrupt Christ's temptations by limiting them to the accounts of His seductions in Matthew 4 and Luke 4. We forget the narrator's final comment that after these tests, the devil "departed from Him until an opportune time" (Luke 4:13). We don't take seriously how much Jesus must have been tempted to "throw in the towel" with His ignorant, sometimes hard-hearted, mistaken, obnoxious disciples, who never seemed to be able to get things right.

Henri Nouwen defines the three main recorded temptations as seductions to be Relevant, Popular through Spectacle, and Powerful.[38] But how much also must He have been tempted to be crabby, impatient, efficient, arrogant, self-centered, or rude! After all, the Letter to Hebrews tell us, He "in every respect has been tested as we are" (4:15a). And lest we corrupt this aspect of Jesus' life on the opposite side and suggest that Jesus probably blew it once in a while, the writer adds "yet without sin" (15b).

Our worst corruption is probably the reduction of the severity of His temptations by our inability to conceive of His total humanity intertwined with His total divinity without any lessening of the former with all its weaknesses. I think His temptations were much more severe than ours precisely because He was constantly lured to be God in His own human way.

After all, the petitions "Thy will be done" and "Lead us not into temptation" are best understood as a pair. Every time we seek to do God's will, it will be a place of temptation for us—to do it for our own reasons or benefit, to gain honor or appreciation, to do it in our own way, to do it falsely. Since Jesus was always doing His Father's will, words, and works, He had to battle every minute to keep doing them all in His Father's way.

I put this segment on temptations here in the book because it seems that at the moment of Christ's most important work for us, He perhaps was the most severely tempted to give up His submission to the Father. The struggle was unquestionably so arduous that I sometimes purposely understate it by suggesting that it would have been a tough temptation not to zap all those jeering Him with a bolt of lightning or two. Not only did He endure the anguished travail of Gethsemane, the mocking crowds and the taunting soldiers, the invitation to prove that He was God by coming down from the cross (except that only by staying crucified would He remain God and true to the character of God), but also that great tempter probably assaulted Him throughout the struggle.

C. S. Lewis imagines it this way through the character of the White Witch as she kills Aslan the Lion, the Son of the Great Emperor:

> At last she drew near. She stood by Aslan's head. Her face was working and twitching with passion, but his looked up at the sky, still quiet, neither angry nor afraid, but a little sad. Then, just before she gave the blow, she stooped down and said in a quivering voice, "And now, who has won? Fool, did you think that by all this you would save the human traitor? Now I will kill you instead of him as our pact was and so the Deep Magic will be appeased. But when you are dead what will prevent me from killing him as well? And who will take him out of my hand *then*? Understand that you have given me Narnia forever; you have lost your own life and you have not saved his. In that knowledge, despair and die."[39]

What great despairs must have filled Jesus' mind as He hung there! Now surely the powers of evil had won. His friends had run away, His poor mother had this enormous shame and sorrow to bear, and, worst of all, His Father had abandoned Him.

No wonder the skies wept and the earth shuddered. For a while, all hell had broken loose.

DYING
(CHRIST ON THE CROSS)

If we really come to grips with the astonishing folly of Christ dying on the cross, we can't corrupt it by trivializing it, singing cutesy or dancey songs about it, reducing it simply to the consequence of His controversial teaching, or, worst of all, ignoring the truth that such folly is *precisely* the way God works in the world.

The cross was the most debasing of shames; the whole point of crucifixion in Roman times was to degrade. As Fleming Rutledge preached, "No other method has ever matched it in terms of public disgust; that was its express purpose."[40] To join ourselves to the folly of Jesus choosing to undergo such a ghastly death willingly, perhaps we ought to wear miniature electric chairs on our neck chains. The only thing so shameful that I can think of is the outrageous treatment in 2004 by U.S. soldiers in the Abu Ghraib prison of Iraqi detainees, whose very Muslim identity was utterly defiled by forcing them into humiliating nakedness and taking lurid photographs of it.

Just as we are horrified by the soldiers' behavior (and the realization that we, having the same nature, could *do* the same), so we should be horrified by the cross, instead of singing about it so glibly. Paul Rowntree Clifford explains well (so I will quote him at length) the immense significance for our lives of a chief dialectic in this folly:

> One of the most striking things about the ministry of Jesus was that he renounced power as that was commonly understood and at the same time claimed divine authority. . . . For the overwhelming majority of people, authority entails the

152

exercise of power understood as enforcement. The disciples of Jesus were as bewildered as anyone else at the refusal of their Master to equate the two and to submit to suffering and death as the way of establishing his authority. For those who believe that nothing is achieved in this world except by compulsion, by forcing other people to submit to their will, the idea that moral authority is more powerful than physical or manipulative force seems wholly unrealistic, if not incomprehensible. But the primitive church had to begin to come to terms with the paradox. Early Christians were helped to do so by their belief in the resurrection. But this did not alter the fact that Jesus had died an ignominious death at the hands of those who continued to wield power. If they were now to acknowledge him as Lord—almost certainly the earliest confession of Christian faith and a denial of the Roman emperor's claim to absolute lordship and authority—they had to start to come to terms with the way in which he exercised authority. And that meant taking the crucifixion seriously. Did it establish a moral authority against which no exercise of political power could ultimately prevail?

That was Paul's conviction, startlingly declared in his first letter to the Corinthian church: "This doctrine of the cross is sheer folly to those on their way to ruin, but to us who are on the way to salvation it is the power of God . . ."[41]

When we realize, as singer Michael Card says, that Christ "loves us so much that he would rather die than live without us,"[42] what can we do in response but enter willingly into the same folly—by believing that God's gracious weakness is stronger than all power, that Christ's submission to unjust atrocities exposed their futility, that non-violence for us too is really the only way to win the war.

GRAVE

It might surprise many to think about how we have distorted the meaning of Christ's grave—but, in truth, we do so frequently by jumping too quickly to the resurrection. We know the story too well, so we don't dwell in the dark of the tomb and acknowledge its finality. Usually we think of Good Friday as the beginning of a three-day chain of events that culminate in resurrection.

However, as Alan E. Lewis explains in *Between Cross and Resurrection*,

> Far from being the first day, the day of the cross is, in the logic of the narrative itself, actually the last day, the end of the story of Jesus. And the day that follows it is not an in-between day which simply waits for the morrow, but it is an empty void, a nothing, shapeless, meaningless, and anticlimactic: simply the day after the end.[43]

As Lewis' book makes very clear, for the sake of ministry in our postmodern, post-Holocaust, post-optimistic, postreligious world, we should pay more attention to that void and recognize the depths of despair in which many people presently live. The Church should spend more time in Holy Saturday contemplation, looking earnestly backwards to the cross and only then forwards to the resurrection—and the two must be constantly kept in dialectical tension.

Instead of meditating more on the grave of Christ, however, churches seem to be running away from its emptiness. Early in the history of the Church, the saints celebrated a long Easter vigil beginning at midnight or in the wee hours of Easter

154

morning. In my childhood we had Easter sunrise services that always began before the light of dawn. In contrast, now most of the churches in my present home city have moved their Easter vigils to early on Saturday evening for the sake of the comfort of the worshipers and an earlier bedtime for children.

I have no right to criticize that move since I'm not the pastor of a local congregation nor the parent of young children, but I do think we lose an important spiritual and emotional experience—waiting in darkness, experiencing the silence of God's death, and pondering life's hopelessness if Christ is not the Messiah we had hoped Him to be.

If we concentrated more on the finality of the grave, we would be more able to give up our useless hopes, our trust in ourselves. We would more compassionately understand our neighbors who are exhausted by the rat race, the never-ending efforts to rescue their lives from insignificance and meaninglessness.

Do we ourselves know how good the Good News is if we don't take seriously a descent into hell? Are we able to bring the Good News to those in despair if we have never walked the Emmaus road wondering how to go on when all our hopes have been dashed? Have we savored the surge of heavenly Joy that ignites us when we discover that the gardener is really our Rabbi or when our eyes are opened to the Stranger who has accompanied us in the darkness and still breaks bread to enlighten us?

SALVATION

Isn't it ironic that a Hebrew word (*yâsha'*, "to open wide or free"), which suggests "plenty of room," has been frequently restricted to tight quarters—and especially that the Creator of salvation has been shifted from the King and Lord of the universe to feeble, fallible human beings?

Some Christians diminish salvation by turning it into merely personal salvation, attainable by our "choosing" to believe. This attitude is epitomized by the song, "*I've decided* to follow Jesus," which doesn't mention at all that we wouldn't even know who He is without the Holy Spirit's teaching, that we wouldn't have known to follow unless He had called us, and that He wouldn't be incarnate to follow without being begotten of the Father. Somehow the entire triune work of salvation has been expunged by our narcissistic penchant for "personal choice."

On the opposite side of the theological spectrum, some Christians turn salvation into our own work by envisioning it solely in terms of our efforts to bring peace and justice to the world—as if we could ever accomplish that impossible work! As the entire biblical testimony makes clear, only by the thorough workings of the Triune God across time will the divine reign culminate in an eternal, cosmic kingdom of total justice and peace.

God wants to save the entire creation! God triunely rescues the world, delivers us from the oppressions of various principalities and powers and counterspirits and evil doers, liberates us from the bondage of our own sinfulness, works in all history and space to bring about the ultimate recapitulation of all that has ever been created. Assemble all the synonyms

156

for salvation—for which there are numerous words in both Testaments of the Scriptures—and we will only begin to grasp the fullness of salvation.

The biblical writers used every image and metaphor, every noun and verb they could imagine to display this indescribable gift. Instead of exulting in our brilliant choosing (such idolatry!), how can we help but fall on our knees in wonder and praise that God should so condescend as to save us. We, one wee part of an infinite conglomeration of rescued ones, receive salvation as gift, sheer gift—brilliant, electrifying, grace-full, compassionate, preposterous, world-quaking, cosmos recapitulating gift.

ATONEMENT

Sometimes I think the word *atonement* is the most controversial term in the Christian vocabulary. Many people nurse deep animosities because of corruptions of the doctrine they experienced in childhood. I remember my shock in an adult Bible class several years ago when I asked what the word *atonement* meant and a prominent church leader erupted, "It means that I'm a terrible sinner and caused Jesus to die for me, so I'd *better* be grateful." She said it with so much venom that I felt poisoned for days after.

She was somewhat right in her anger, of course. Many churches pour on the guilt about our sinfulness so thickly that there is hardly any room for gratitude. To teach about sin without going overboard requires great sensitivity, compassion, and skill—but still the recognition of our sinfulness is a necessary component of any discussion of atonement.

Over the course of the Church's history different aspects of the complicated biblical picture of atonement have been highlighted. Primarily three images have been accentuated—Jesus' victory over the powers of evil (the *Christus Victor* metaphor prominent especially in the age of Constantine and other empires and most clearly enunciated by Gustav Aulén), Jesus as Substitute under God's judgment (most thoroughly elaborated by Anselm of Canterbury in the medieval period), and Jesus as Model or Moral Influence for the godly life (the so-called "subjective view" affiliated with Abelard in the Middle Ages).

These three themes offer us important insights so we will look at each in separate sections below; however, these metaphors and all the rest in the Scriptures are insufficient by themselves so we can let the gifts of one correct the inadequacies of another.[44] Most of our corruptions of atonement arise because an overemphasis on one theme or another stretches that analogy past its breaking point so that it becomes unbiblical.[45]

Sometimes distortions arise because people want to avoid one biblical image or another; often the result is a falsifying of atonement entirely. We must always ask the question, "Why did Jesus *have* to die on the cross?" To limit atonement to understandable metaphors, as some try to do, is often to remove the necessity for the cross entirely.

We have to remember that metaphors cannot be too tightly pinned down. They are suggestive. Eugene Peterson, in his "Foreword" to a book on preaching with reference to the music of the acclaimed rock band U2, reminds us that

> when used as a metaphor, a word explodes into life—it starts *moving*. . . . Metaphor . . . makes me a participant in creating the meaning and entering into the action of the word. . . . When metaphor is banished and language is bullied into serving as mere information and definition, as happens so often in our computerized culture and cultural religion, the life goes out of the language. It also goes out of us. When this reduction happens in relation to God and all that pertains to God, we end up sitting around having study and discussion groups in religious museums.[46]

My goal in looking at some of the images and metaphors used in the Scriptures for atonement is that we can retain the life of words frequently discarded these days by letting those words *move* around in our brains and hearts. May the end result be more gratitude above all.

Two professors from a Mennonite seminary and a Methodist seminary offer together the following three useful points of orientation for all our thinking about the atonement;

> *First, we see in Scripture and have come to believe that God and his ways cannot be understood fully nor in any way circumscribed by the models, images and words we have chosen. . . . Second, our commitment to the Scriptures of the Old and New Testaments as*

> *the Scriptures of the church provide us with room to maneuver*
> *as well as with a limit to our maneuvering. . . . Finally, we believe*
> *that the Holy Spirit works through the community of God's people*
> *in a way that is both creative and cautionary.*[47]

These guidelines should be kept in mind, it seems to me, in all our doctrinal wrestlings.

Another source for corruptions of the doctrine of atonement or for rejections of various metaphors is an inadequate trinitarianism, which might, for example, picture Jesus as receiving the wrath of His Father without any acknowledgement of the entire Trinity's participation as "judged judge." Over the past few years as I have been studying the subject, I have found that often artists capture the sense of the Scriptures better than those who analyze, especially when our theories come out of our own mind, rather than out of adoration and reverence.

For example, in an art museum in Columbia, South Carolina, I encountered a painting from around 1520 from the studio of Tintoretto (perhaps from the master himself) which shows the entire Trinity on the cross. Similarly, at the Burrell Collection in Glasgow, Scotland, there is an English (from Nottingham) painted alabaster carving of the Trinity from around 1375–85, which depicts the Father sorrowfully holding the Son with the Spirit as a dove nearby. A wool and linen altar frontal, "The Holy Trinity, with St. John, the Virgin, and the Angels" from Nürnberg in South Germany around 1420 includes not only the wounded Three, but also a pennant hanging from the cross and containing three symbols (too far away for me to see if they were crosses or scrolls) and what seemed to be a phoenix. All three of these works of art, more thoroughly than many sermons I've heard, showed the immense cost to all three persons in the Godhead of our atonement. They portrayed in oils, stone, and fabrics what the Orthodox call the triune *perichoresis*, the full, mutual communion of Father, Son, and Spirit for the sake of the salvation of the cosmos.

Who can even begin to comprehend such amazing love? All we can do with the mystery of the atonement is respond with our best art and adoration and acceptance.

CHRISTUS VICTOR

This metaphor of atonement emphasizes that at the cross Jesus defeated all the powers of evil, including Satan and his forces, as well as oppressive governments, Mammon, misconstrued religions, and death. Church father Athanasius makes use of this image in writing, "Death came to His body, therefore, not from Himself but from enemy action, in order that the Saviour might utterly abolish death in whatever form they offered it to Him."[48]

One great gift of the *Christus Victor* theme for our understanding is that it emphasizes the triumph of the atonement. God in Christ is especially seen as a warrior who conquers evil and liberates human beings from their captivity to all the powers.

One corruption of this theme arises if people see themselves only as victims of evil and not as perpetrators of it—a distortion highlighted in the comic line, "the devil made me do it." It's true that we often become captives of the powers, but usually we've first let them become gods in our lives. Since our society specializes in victimization, this theme finds ready adherents among those eager to relieve themselves of responsibility for their own lives.

Another corruption emanates not from our experience as hostages to the powers, but from our extrapolation that since we are co-conquerors with Christ we can take on the vengeance which the Bible reserves for God, the only One who can righteously vent it. This is illustrated most horribly by the folk who engaged in the Crusades or who wage pre-emptive wars on the presumption that Christ's followers are warriors who must secure His victories and liberate the Holy Land or root out evil in other nations.

We'll get Christ's victory over evil forces right only if we remember that He accomplished it by submitting to them and taking their violence into Himself. Christ Himself will bring about the ultimate defeat of the powers, and in the meanwhile His victory sets us free from their enslavements. Consequently, we *stand* against the powers (Eph. 6:11, 13, 14)—never forgetting that we share with them a propensity instead to act violently out of our fallenness.[49] Then we will accept our proper responsibility for peacemaking discipleship without assuming that we have the right to be violent in Christ's name.

SUBSTITUTION
(CHRIST'S VICARIOUS ATONEMENT)

In these short attempts to reclaim corrupted words it is impossible to describe thoroughly the prominent theories of the atonement or to list all the corruptions. I offer only brief sketches and hope thereby to whet our appetites for more adequate study and less hasty rejection of biblical images. Perhaps in no case is this more necessary than with the metaphor of Christ as Substitute for us under the judgment of God (hinted at in 2 Cor. 5:21 and 1 Thess. 5:9–10).

Many scholars think this metaphor is no longer suitable in contemporary times since, they insist, people are not still haunted by guilt and condemnation as were medieval peasants and obsessed reformers like Martin Luther.[50] I disagree, for I constantly meet people who regret things they've said or done. To corrupt this biblical theme by neglect is to ignore the realities of everyday life. People might not fear *God's* condemnation, but they certainly condemn themselves and constantly battle their feelings of remorse and guilt. I have seen the look of sheer relief on their faces and heard it in their expressions of gratitude after forgiveness has been announced.

Leon Morris, whose *The Cross in the New Testament* discusses all the New Testament passages regarding atonement and explicates the early Church's teachings, emphasizes both the unity and variety of themes. He also insists "that there is a much more solid weight of scriptural teaching behind the view that Christ was in some sense our Substitute than most modern scholars will allow."[51]

We've noted previously that the Substitution metaphor is also corrupted by those who overstate the guilt and neglect both the grace of forgiveness and the goodness of God's delight in us as His beloved creation. God is Judge over us unquestionably, but God also came off the bench triunely to take His own punishment. We are rebels and offenders truly, but we are also forgiven and given Christ's own righteousness. We are blameworthy indeed, but God's free gifts to us are grace to deal with our sin and peace to remove our guilt.

PROPITIATION

This biblical word (*hilasmos*) has been corrupted in our time by being totally rejected. Contemporary translations omit it entirely in favor of less problematic words like *expiation* or the phrase *sacrifice of atonement* (Rom. 3:25 and 1 John 2:2, 4:10). The former is too impersonal—a person expiates by making amends. The latter is too vague; though it is important to recognize that Christ offered Himself as a sacrifice to make our atonement possible, the phrase does not show that what His sacrifice did was turn away the wrath of God.

That idea makes us queasy these days. We modern people simply don't like the notion that Christ's atoning work necessarily turned away God's anger.

Many of the people who retain that idea, however, mix up the focus of God's wrath and think that it was directed toward Christ. This misunderstanding draws the appropriate feminist critique that it turns the Father into a patriarchal oppressor of the Son.

If we maintain a biblical trinitarianism, though, we realize that throughout the Scriptures God has restrained the divine wrath again and again at expense to God's self. The Lord's wrath is thoroughly righteous, absolutely necessary for the well-being of the cosmos, for it is directed against everything and every action and everyone that harm the triune Creator's good creation. God is not only "incurably loving," but God is also "implacably opposed to evil."[52]

I think the reason that we don't like the idea of "propitiation" these days is because we really don't like to admit that we are such consorts with, and workers of, evil that God should have to suffer so to bear His own wrath against our wickedness. The words *evil* and *wicked* are just not terms we usually apply to ourselves, but if propitiation was necessary—and the Bible insists it was—then we better face the fact that those adjectives describe us quite truly.

Then another deep layer is added to our understanding of atonement: namely, that on the cross Jesus took into Himself all the (physical, emotional, spiritual, social) pain of justifiable divine wrath in order to turn it away from us. By doing so, Jesus was actually assenting to the righteousness of God's anger against sin and agreeing to swallow it Himself, rather than let it fall upon us and drown us. Moreover, if we are truly trinitarian, we realize that the Father and Spirit bore the anguish within themselves, too (though not in bodily form).

Why would we let our own prideful inability to admit our own odious destitution prevent us from rejoicing in the immensity of this inexplicable mercy: that the Triune God chooses to ingest and endure His own wrath?

RANSOM, REDEMPTION, SACRIFICE

We corrupt these words when we try to explain *how* Jesus redeemed us or bought us back and *to whom* Jesus paid the ransom fee or sacrificed Himself. That effort to clarify what is incomprehensible, however, goes beyond the biblical testimony. The Scriptures say simply that Christ was a ransom for many (Matt. 20:28, Mark 10:45, 1 Tim. 2:6) and that we were ransomed *from* our futile ways (1 Peter 1:18) and ransomed *for* God (Rev. 5:9). Similarly, Christ came to redeem those *under* the Law (Gal. 4:5) and to redeem us *from* iniquity (Titus 2:14) or the curse of the Law (Gal. 3:13). Past tense uses of *redeemed* interchange "God" and "Christ" as the subject (Luke 1:68, Gal. 3:13) and celebrate that we have been bought back from the earth and from humankind in order to be first fruits for God and the Lamb (Rev. 14:3, 4). The name *Redeemer* is never given to Christ in the New Testament, but many instances in the First Testament should convince those who think Jesus had to pay God that instead the whole Trinity's character is to redeem.

The idea of sacrificing gives us some hints as to how redemption works, but not enough for us to think we understand this immense mystery. Romans 3:25 tells us that "God put [Jesus] forward as a sacrifice of atonement ('propitiation') by His blood," even as 1 John 4:10 reports that "God sent His Son to be the atoning sacrifice ('propitiation')." But lest we think these texts hint at patriarchal sadism, Ephesians 5:2 and Hebrews 9:26 proclaim that Jesus willingly gave Himself as a sacrifice to God to remove sin. After His sacrifice He sat down at God's right hand, the place of fellowship (Heb. 10:12). Being both the sacrifice and in the triune fellowship, Jesus can be the mediator for us (1 John 2:2).

I don't know about you, but the idea of Jesus as a ransom and sacrifice doesn't repel me; instead it stuns me with the scandalous immensity of His love that I should be the pearl for which He, the merchant of the kingdom of heaven, sells all that He has, Himself, that I might be His own (Matt. 13:45–46).

As a result, the kingdom of heaven is to me like a treasure hidden, and in its sublime Joy I want to sell all that I have to secure it (Matt. 13:44). Christ's sacrifice empowers me to offer myself within the Church as a living sacrifice to God (Rom. 12:1), to offer gladness and praise that God should go to such lengths on our behalf.

REDEMPTION

We'll look at the word *redemption* again because the word not only connotes paying a price to buy us back from our captivity to ourselves and the world's evil, but the word is also used as a general term to summarize all that the Trinity has done for us to make us God's own.

The word has been abused and corrupted mostly by those who turn redemption into cheap grace—God rescues me and makes me cozy and safe, secure in my assurance of heaven. This reduction usually makes the whole job quite easy for God and for us. Not much depth is given to the extremity to which God went on our behalf, and redemption doesn't seem in this corruption to require anything from us in response. Even worse, the response is often a smug "I'm saved; are you?" superiority over those who don't know the magic words to secure this state.

On the other hand, redemption can become too costly for us in the minds of those who insist that redemption cannot be ours unless we have confessed each and every little sin (as if we could ever recognize them all!). I have been told by many that I'm obviously not fully redeemed because I have multiple health handicaps. What sins in my life have I failed to confess that I still struggle with these issues? Redemption becomes something I have to earn by the diligence of my confession and the thoroughness of my repentance.

Then there is the corruption of redemption by those who won't admit how much we need it. These are the people who trust human beings to be able to fix themselves, to escape from the bondage of sin and decay to which we are subject and to accomplish self improvement and, therefore, secure our own ticket into eternal bliss.

All of these corruptions can fail to recognize that God's redemption is so thorough that we become the Trinity's agents, pouring out our own lives, too, to invite others into triune freedom. Evelyn Underhill summarizes this well in this excerpt from her retreat notes:

> Redemption does not mean you and me made safe and popped into heaven. It means that each soul, redeemed from self interest by the revelation of Divine Love, is taken and used again for the spread of that redeeming work. It gives us a sort of measure of our own spiritual state, the degree of our real effectiveness, if we consider what, plunged in the real world of spirit, our first instinctive action would be. Should we want to exert power and love for the redemption of others, or should we ask and need those gifts for ourselves? Should we first remember our own helplessness and dependence, or should we be so deeply at one with the Divine Love that all we care about is to spend and redeem?[53]

Are we really redeemed (especially from our own self interest) if we are not passionate about passing on the fullness of God's love to those who do not yet know infinite spiritual freedom?

Moreover, this passing on of redemption occurs primarily because of our intense Joy, the exhilaration of having stored up "the supernatural sunshine" so that we "can spend it again on others" (69). Saint Francis is a great model of such celestial Joy, such eagerness to spread redemption. And this was possible for him because he and other saints have "most fully accepted the mystery of the Cross and therefore have drawn nearest to God" and therefore they understand and experience most deeply this heavenly Joy (69).

For many of us who tend to be too hard on ourselves, the great delight of redemption is that it frees us from our own "self-centered attitude towards perfection," which, Underhill scoffs is "not humility but stupidity." She stresses that we come into God's presence "to open ourselves to the beauty and harmony offered us by God in Christ, to learn more surrender

and adoration, *not* just to scrape and sandpaper ourselves."
God redeems us from such self flagellation with "mercy and
gentleness" (56).

Then the incredible fullness of that redeeming grace fills
us with true humility—and wonder and a flaming eternal Joy
so intense that it burns up our sandpaper!

SLAIN LAMB

Some contemporary theologians reject entirely the idea of the Lamb who was slaughtered, the necessity of Christ dying as a sacrifice. A lesser corruption is to see the image as a mere metaphor and not take seriously how necessary it was in the Trinity's whole plan for Israel and the entire cosmos that Jesus should bring to completion the First Testament commandment of blood sacrifices for sin (see especially Leviticus 4, 5, and 16). Furthermore, Jesus as the slain Lamb should bring to our minds the Passover Lamb, whose blood was painted on the lintels of Israelites' homes so that they would be delivered from the Angel of Death (Exodus 12). These two dimensions of His being slain are brought together in 1 Corinthians 5:7b–8, "For our paschal lamb, Christ, has been sacrificed. Therefore let us celebrate the festival . . ."

It seems strange to *celebrate* Christ's blood, but that is exactly what Jesus invites us to do when He commands the disciples at the Last Supper to "do this in remembrance of me," for "This cup that is poured out for you is the new covenant in my blood" (Luke 22:19–20).

For me the celebration of the Last Supper is a richly eternal feast that knits together the past, present, and future in a seamless whole. Jesus has told us not only that we should remember His enormous gift to us in the past, but also that as we participate in the meal now we proclaim His death in the present. This connection is graphically illustrated by the crucifixion scene of the Isenheim Altarpiece by Matthias Grünewald, which includes John the Baptizer pointing (with an exaggerated finger) to Christ hanging on the cross. Next to John stands a Lamb, "bleeding into a communion chalice and reminding us in unmistakable terms that the excruciating suffering that we see on the Cross is 'to take away the sin of the world.'"[54] When we eat and drink at His supper, we are also commissioned as John to give witness daily to the way God works through suffering by our own words and lives for the sake of our neighbors.

Moreover, as Paul reminds us in 1 Corinthians 11:17–34, when we eat together in the community we participate in Christ's own Body, the Church, even as we receive His body and blood with all their gifts. This also includes a responsibility, for we are called to "discern the body" and, as the context at Corinth teaches us, that means we ought never to lose sight of the poor. Could our eucharistic feasts be carried by us all more thoroughly into our daily lives, so that all our meals challenge us to share our bread with the needy?

And then there is all the fullness of tomorrow in this Supper. It gives us a foretaste of the future feast, the wedding supper of the Lamb. The Book of Revelation ties this supper together with the necessity for the Lamb to have been slaughtered, so that we realize that the Bridegroom's bloody invitation cleanses His Bride, the Church (as in Eph. 5:25–28).

Preacher Fleming Rutledge adds to these biblical conceptions the fulfillment in Jesus of Abraham's promise to Isaac, "God will provide himself *the lamb* for a burnt offering, my son" (Gen. 22:1–19). The incredible facet of that gift is that it was given with the full acceptance by the Son of the Father's will. As Rutledge summarizes,

As the apocalyptic, conquering lamb he defeats sin, stamps it out, eradicates it. As the Paschal lamb he stands between us and the specter of Death. As the sacrificial lamb he gives his own blood to be the *once-for-all* offering to cleanse his own from sin for ever. Yes, once for all: *ephapax* in Greek, a word repeated in Hebrews four times for emphasis. The sheer, utter, final efficacy of Christ's self-offering is underlined by Thomas Cranmer's Eucharistic words: "his one oblation of himself once offered, a full, perfect and sufficient sacrifice . . ." (65)

173

This slain Lamb is the foundation of the world, as the character Alyosha reveals in Fyodor Dostoevsky's *The Brothers Karamazov*.[55] The novel makes clear through Alyosha's new brotherhood with the boys that the only possible basis for true community is the forgiveness secured by Christ's sacrifice.

Do we receive and build our lives on that gift?

As Fleming Rutledge proclaims, John the Baptizer keeps calling us to "Behold" this Lamb of God. And she woos us with this glorious conclusion to her sermon:

> The point [of the sermon] is that you behold and believe that you yourself are one for whom Christ died. In this Holy Week preaching, it is not the preacher that reaches out for you. It is the Word of God reaching out for you in Jesus Christ. It is your sin, not just someone else's, that is taken away in his sacrifice of himself. It is you who are "washed in the blood of the Lamb." It is you who, like Isaac, have been snatched back from the very brink of the grave by the One who has provided his own Lamb as a substitute. It is you who have heard, tonight, how God has made the Great Exchange, becoming an offering for sin so that you might receive new life and new righteousness in him. Behold: the Lamb of God. (66)

Once again, the arts capture the biblical significance better than our theological ruminations can. Rutledge reminds of this hymn, one of my favorites:

> At the Lamb's high feast we sing
> Praise to our victorious king,
> Who has washed us in the tide
> Flowing from his pierced side. Alleluia!
>
> Praise we him, whose love divine
> Gives his sacred blood for wine,
> Gives his body for the feast—
> Christ the victim, Christ the priest. Alleluia!
>
> Where the paschal blood is poured
> Death's dread angel sheathes the sword;
> Israel's hosts triumphant go
> Through the way that drowns the foe. Alleluia!

Praise we Christ, whose blood was shed,
Paschal victim, paschal bread;
With sincerity and love
Eat we manna from above. Alleluia!

Mighty Victim from the sky,
Hell's fierce pow'rs beneath you lie;
You have conquered in the fight,
You have brought us life and light. Alleluia! . . .[56]

Who could imagine that such a bloody victim could bring us such mingled sorrow, repentance, and exhilarating, eschatological Joy?

JUSTIFICATION

Here is a word, signifying God's constant action of making things right, that many people want to discard—insisting that we ought not to use such theological jargon. They assert that theological truths must be put into the common language of people. This argument is wrong for two reasons: first, because the terms *to justify* and *justification* are commonly used in our time and the behavior of self-justification is universal and prevalent, and second, because the word connotes an action of God that is supremely important for our understanding of genuine freedom.

Let me justify my first point first. Business travelers must justify their expense accounts to prove that the expenditures listed are reasonable or necessary in pursuit of their work. Writers must (or need not) "justify the margins" of their manuscripts, and almost all books are printed with justified margins.

The action of justification is common conduct. Many of the children in my husband's former fifth-grade classes worked harder to justify their misbehaviors than they worked on their homework. And we all seem to wind up trying to justify our existence at parties. The customary question "What do you do?" makes it necessary to prove that our presence is worthwhile. Why would people say such things as "I'm just a homemaker" if our society's ridiculous ethos of "corporate success" didn't produce the (unjustifiable) sense that such an honorable occupation is less than justifiable?

The actions of trying to justify ourselves and the word *justification* are common enough, so we don't have to corrupt the theological doctrine by any refusal to use it. A more invidious distortion occurs, however, when we use the terms but deny the reality. We falsify God's gift of justification when we refuse to let God do the justifying. Perhaps for many of us this is our pet sin.

Why do some of us have such trouble truly believing that God has broken down all the barriers between us and Himself? Why do we keep feeling guilty even though we know (or do we?) that we are forgiven? Why do we keep acting as if we had to prove ourselves, to justify our worth for the sake of others' approval?

If we believe that God has completely justified us in Christ and by His inexplicable work of atonement, then why do we not live in greater freedom, the comfort and liberty of truly being ourselves, filled with the Spirit and acting out of triune grace?

Of course, this opposite corruption is equally horrendous: that we should live as if "God likes to forgive, and I like to sin; isn't that a nice arrangement?" When we so take God's gift of justification for granted, then we deny the very love that makes it possible and throw it back in God's face. This corruption appears as a cavalier "once saved; always saved" attitude or in a misplaced confidence in one's baptism or confirmation to be sufficient, regardless of one's present relationship with God.

Lutherans have particularly been prone to this posture (often described as a "forensic" conception in which justification appears to be only a nominal and external verdict by God) because of misconstruals of Martin Luther's writings on justification. Recent studies of his work by Finnish scholars, however, have shown that Luther understood far more deeply than is usually acknowledged that justification calls forth life in union with Christ, that it entails participation in God's life.[57] Beyond a juridical imputation of righteousness is actual adoption into the Sonship of Jesus in which we dwell.

What a wonder it would be if we who follow Christ could really learn the freedom of justification. Then, liberated from our hopeless attempts to fix ourselves, we would no longer need to validate ourselves or try to impress others. In humility we would know our propensity to sin, but in gratitude we would know the power of grace to prevent it. Then, fully dependent upon forgiveness and the Spirit's love poured into us, we would live in exuberant and radiant obedience to God. This is a vision of true freedom worth living by.

Why would anyone want to get along without God's justification, the Trinity's constant action of making things right? In Christ God accomplished justification for the cosmos once for all, but we need it afresh every minute.

SANCTIFICATION

One of the reasons that God's "justification" is often misunderstood is that it is separated too widely from "sanctification." The latter is also a term that many want to throw out as meaningless jargon, and the word has been further corrupted by the exaggerated piety of sanctimonious people,[58] who pretend to a holiness that no one except Jesus could possibly live.

The greatest distortion of sanctification occurs when we start to think that we accomplish it ourselves—that we can fix ourselves, get rid of our tendency to sin, make ourselves more holy, attain perfection. Of course it is true that holiness is nourished by our participation in the practices of the faith,[59] but it is *God's work* through those practices that enables us more to act like the saints that we are by virtue of God's justification of us. The same God who forgives our sins also sets us free from their controlling power.

Holiness is not abstract. It is the story of God's multifaceted interventions in the world.[60]

Another, more subtle, corruption of sanctification arises when one's piety is not rooted in the dialectical combination of truth and love. This can be seen in the warped "holiness" of those who insist on God's commands as the basis for moral deliberations, but do so without love for their opponents. On the opposite side are those who emphasize love, but lose the truth of the Scriptures.

Jesus demonstrated true holiness when He said to the woman caught in adultery, "Neither do I condemn you. Go your way, and from now on do not sin again" (John 8:11). He did not dismiss the actuality of sin (in which she might have

179

been an unwilling participant), but forgives her in love and by grace sets her free for fresh obedience.

In the past I have thought about justification and sanctification primarily as a first and second step in God's work for and in us. Now, I see them more as two sides of the same coin, which landed first on the justification side as Christ accomplished the sacrifice of atonement that forgives us. Thereafter, the coin keeps spinning as the two actions of God continually reinforce each other. We can't be open to God's renewing, sanctifying work within us if we don't know clearly that we are forgiven, but when we fail and think, say, or do things contrary to God's best way, the opulence of triune forgiveness widens us to receive more of God's sanctifying work.

That is one of the reasons I love Sunday morning worship so much. Sometimes I have trouble forgiving myself and digging out of the guilt I feel because I'm not the kind and gracious person I'd like to be. Then in worship, when I hear the pastor or priest announce to me the entire forgiveness of all my sin, it tastes so good that it makes me hungry for holiness. And the texts and sermon, music and liturgy, liturgical symbols and sacraments, and community keep teaching me about a God who wants to—and will!—work it in me. What a feast!

MODEL (MORAL EXAMPLE)

The third most prominent metaphor for atonement, besides *Christus Victor* over the powers and Substitute for us under God's judgment, is that Jesus is the Model for us, the Moral Example which we are to follow. As with the other images noted above, this one also has strong biblical foundations. Jesus certainly was/is a prophetic Teacher, whose gospel pronouncements enlighten us, especially concerning God's kingdom and our ministries within it to preach, heal, and make peace.

Moreover, Jesus was/is a great Lover, who shows us how to nourish deep (non-genital) friendships with both men and women. His love overcomes the weakness of our own and inspires us to greater heights of adoration for God and compassion for our neighbors, even as His teaching spurs us to greater zeal in pursuing the kingdom way of life. This, of course, will involve suffering—not just suffering in imitation of Christ, but, because we are adopted into the triune family, we actually share in Christ's suffering (see Col. 1:24). This is why Lent is so important so that we are trained to be willing to bear it.

This morning on National Public Radio I heard a report of an Adventist missionary and a Hutu orphanage director who both risked their lives to save many people, both Hutus and Tutsis, children and adults, from the horrendous massacre ten years ago in Rwanda. The missionary especially claimed the model of Jesus as the motivation for his courage and willingness to die. That is the strength of this image for atonement—but it doesn't tell us how our sins are actually forgiven.

That Jesus is our exemplar is a favored metaphor for those who don't like to think about our human sin needing forgiveness or our character needing changing away from its sinful self-orientation. It is also favored by those who think any talk of principalities and powers is a leftover archaism from an outdated ancient cosmology.

That very select status demonstrates a glaring weakness in the image. How do we get the courage to live like Jesus if we don't have His character? The whole idea that we could fix ourselves and become like Him trivializes the evil in which we are enmeshed. How do we resist systemic evil if we don't recognize its deep underpinnings in good creations overstepping their proper vocations?[61]

More deeply, we can't follow Jesus' example because we are incapable of His holy obedience. As Colin Gunton deftly points out, "Jesus is an example because he and he alone is the incarnate Son who by the enabling of the Holy Spirit remained unfallen . . . His humanity is only what it is because it is that of the one sent by the Father through the Spirit."[62]

The metaphor is also favored by the "What Would Jesus Do?"–bracelet–wearing crowd. One corruption that appears in this camp is a personalizing of the model so that we don't discern the political implications of Jesus' example. And how many of us, as Jesus did for the Jews, would really go to our deaths in order to avert or at least postpone a war against an oppressed people (like the Iraqis or Palestinians)?

We can't develop Jesus' holiness on our own. We need Him to be made sin for us, so that we might become the righteousness of God in Him (2 Cor. 5:21) by means of His victory, sacrificial substitution, propitiation, forgiveness, justification, sanctification, and reconciliation.

RECONCILIATION

Sometimes the word *reconciliation* is used in place of other images of atonement because it sounds less drastic, doesn't seem to need the sacrifice of Jesus, needn't imply God's judgment on human sin, or doesn't seem to put so much blame on us. But anyone who thinks that way must not be using a very serious breach in relationships as an example. Little misunderstandings in a friendship might be easily resolved, but what about the betrayal of a wife by her adulterous husband? To effect reconciliation there would cost plenty for everyone concerned.

So the word can't be watered down. For Jesus to make possible our reconciliation to God still requires Christ's life, suffering, death; in fact, it also requires the involvement of the whole Trinity.

Another corruption of reconciliation arises when people theorize that an angry Father needed to be appeased by the Son in order to be reconciled to sinful human beings. This is to turn everything backwards, for the Trinity was always—even before creation—ready to make it possible for us to be reconciled to God, but we were the ones to turn away.

William Placher offers us this lovely explanation of the meaning of God's wrath and of Christ's willingness to offer Himself for God's reconciling work:

We were running away from God, looking for a place to hide [as Adam and Eve hid in the garden], and we found that God was running beside us, sharing our fear and shame. The sense that we had irreparably damaged our relation with God disappears, and we can stop running away. *We* have been reconciled—God loved us all along, and what needed fixing was the way we had turned away from God. Yet God's love really did take the form of wrath as long as we were alone in the place of sin—"wrath" here not referring to an emotional reaction on the part of God, but functioning as the only way to describe the broken relation from God's side.[63]

The most serious problem with the image of reconciliation is that we can't seem to take its implications seriously. If Jesus Christ runs alongside us as we run away from God in order to bear our pain and then entrusts to us the same ministry of reconciliation in the world, why do we not engage in greater companionship with parties at odds with each other?

Many of our churches can't even reconcile warring factions over styles of worship,[64] much less run alongside the poor of the U.S. who are getting poorer while the rich are getting richer.[65]

John Perkins, the founder of Voice of Calvary Ministries in Mississippi (and of other ministries and services in California), returned to the site of his being beaten in order to bring reconciliation between blacks and whites. In his writings, he stresses that we won't be able to bring about any reconciliation between races and classes or any just redistribution of wealth unless we are willing to relocate and live with those who are oppressed.[66]

Similarly, Hakim Hasan has developed an "Urban Dialogues Seminar Series" because he discovered that the academics who wrote about justice and the people who searched for public policies to change the situation of the urban poor never included them in their discussions and didn't know any working class people as friends.[67] Could churches take more seriously their commission to carry on the ministry of reconciliation and sponsor discussions between the local poor and the local authorities?

What if U.S. Christians had done the hard work of repentance and genuine reconciliation rather than supporting a "war on terror" that only makes militants more eager to attack us? Why do we think that power is the only way to solve problems?

Don't we know that the only way to turn enemies from their hostility is to turn them into friends? Can't we see that reconciliation truly takes running alongside with compassion and genuine love? Would we be willing to pay the price Jesus did for global reconciliation to take place?

THE SCANDAL
(OF CHRIST'S WORK)

It seems that various critics of atonement language in general or of specific metaphors in particular are simply refusing to accept the scandal of who God is in Christ. The result is that all that the Trinity has done for us (and continues to do) is corrupted by an arrogant reduction.

We need some sort of large word to encompass all the things we've been saying about Christ's work of atonement on our behalf, for certainly it includes many aspects of His life, sufferings, and death, His resurrection, ascension, and sending of the Spirit. All these are of a piece, with interlocking meanings and reinforcing images.[68] We can't isolate a few words as some do and imagine that we understand it all. Indeed, the entire truth of what the Triune God is and does for us is so vastly beyond us all that we ought to bow in humble submission and ponder eternally every word and phrase the Bible gives us to think about it.

If we could understand the atonement, we would be God. If we refuse to accept God's metaphors, we are ideological egotists whose prejudices against certain words reveal our silly presuppositions and our tragic refusal to receive the immense scandal of **GOD**

Just one passage, for example, offers many suggestions of ways to contemplate God's prodigious gifts in Christ. In 2 Corinthians 5:14–21, these facets of the divine jewel are specified: vicarious substitution (14–15), change of perspective (16), new creation (17), reconciliation (18–20), forgiveness

(19), representation or interchange (14, 21), sacrifice (21), justification (20–21).

The scandal is that *something* had to have actually removed our sin and guilt; otherwise *where* does the sin go? Does it simply wander off into the wilderness with a goat so that we can ignore it, or are we actually forgiven?

Again, the scandal is that we need actually to be brought back to God. We need a Mediator who doesn't simply give directions, but who *is* the Way, who brings us back.

Again, the scandal is that *somehow* we have to be freed from the powers that enslave us, to be somehow empowered to live differently.

In his *Preface to Theology*, John Howard Yoder sketches eleven words or concepts that must be considered when contemplating the fullness of the atonement and concludes that any theory that we might formulate from pondering these and other biblical ideas must do justice to all the biblical materials and must sufficiently answer the questions, "Why did Jesus have to die?"[69] and "What did His death achieve and how did it do that?"[70]

Over the past four months I've experienced some physical setbacks that have brought these eleven aspects and several others more sharply into focus for me. As always, the analogies can't be stretched too far or they'll snap, but perhaps the following illustration might be useful to a few readers for holding diverse ideas of atonement together. The major problem, of course, is that these are listed in a sequence, whereas atonement, in the fullness of its simultaneous interconnections, can't be put on a timeline.

1) The first element to note is that I critically burned my foot—and we aren't sure how, though we suspect that, unknowingly, it was too close to the heating vent on the floor as I read in my husband's study. That my nerves no longer register pain on the surface of the skin is due to longterm dependence on insulin, necessitated by a measles virus which killed the pancreas when I was a teenager. In the same way, we human beings have lost our ability to function as created for good. We are prone to sin, just as I am prone to foot injuries. We are not able to free ourselves from this bondage to sin, just as I

can't notice when I'm causing myself trouble. We never knew my foot was so badly burned until I awoke the next morning with a 2 1/2" blister and five little ones. In our human life, all sorts of indications—frenzy, bad mistakes, spoiled relationships, inner unease, and so forth—help us see that we are in trouble and need help from outside ourselves.

2) I took oral antibiotics from the beginning, but they couldn't whip the infection that developed in my foot and then spread. I had to be hospitalized for intravenous antibiotics in order to take away that infection. Similarly, we might try to solve our sin problem by ourselves, but we simply can't manage it. As humans we need Someone from outside ourselves to take away our guilt. As our *Substitute*, Christ by proxy took our unrighteousness by means of His voluntary suffering, His vicarious offering of Himself.

3) No healing could take place until the dead skin was eliminated; at the hospital a therapist gave me whirlpool treatments to debride the ruined skin. In the same way, we need a *Christus Victor* to defeat all the powers that hold us captive, especially death. There can be no new life for us sinners unless we are freed from our bondage to death, money, power, and other principalities.

4) After the dead skin was cleansed away I was astonished at how new skin grew on the bottom of my foot—from the inside out. Now after all these months, I am surprised by the gift of that new skin life. Comparably, there needs to be a change within ourselves, *a victory over self* and our self-centeredness, a rebirth into new life. This takes place when we die with Christ and rise with Him into a new creation.

5) By the time the infection was defeated and the foot was completely healed (it took ten weeks), my leg brace no longer fit properly (since the leg muscles have atrophied considerably). An orthotist had to build an entirely new brace so that my leg and foot would have a proper fit, just as God took the initiative in Christ to *reconcile* us to Himself because we human beings couldn't make things right ourselves.

6) One of the worst things about handicaps is that a person feels so alone. During the last months of escalating problems, I was encouraged by friends and participants at speaking en-

gagements who promised me their prayers on my behalf. This was a momentously precious revelation of love. This reminded me, but contrasted profoundly with the *revelation of love* by God in Christ on the cross. The dissimilarity arises because Christ's love is shown to be both extreme and perfect—that He would go to such lengths for our sake is overwhelming to me. As 1 John 3:16 stresses, "We know love by this, that He laid down His life for us—and we ought to lay down our lives for one another." Most of us are not really willing to render up our lives for others, but the cross provides us with a supreme *Model*.

7, 8) During the healing of the large burn on the bottom of my foot, I had to sacrifice walking in order for the skin to heal. That was a necessary sacrifice, but a costly one in that the bones degenerated since there was no pressure on them. Consequently, when I first began to walk again, the heel bones broke. A very red heel both announced the damage and displayed the healing work of extra blood to rebuild my bones. Similarly, so that we could be healed Jesus paid the supreme *ransom* and sacrificed His life. Thereby He created *the new covenant in His blood* which completely remakes us.

9) I had no idea when my attempts to walk were extremely painful that it was because my foot was broken. X-rays, however, showed the truth—and a comparison with an older x-ray made it clear that one of the four screws holding my foot together for the past 15 years was pushing on the broken bones. Now an entirely different sort of healing was shown to be necessary. More thoroughly, the cross of Christ continues to *reveal God's righteousness*—not that Christ was bearing the Trinity's punishment, but that He agreed to God's righteousness and voluntarily submitted Himself to it for our sake. That revelation exposes how much our lives need restoration.

10) The revelation of the state of my foot necessitated that the podiatrist remove the screw that was impacting the broken bones. Again, this process had to be done by someone outside of me. Similarly, the cross alone is able to make things right between us and God; it alone can *justify* us.

11) Once the screw was out, there were not only bones, but a new wound to heal. Here we go again rehealing my

foot skin, I thought. It reminded me of the whole notion of *redemption*, that God had to buy us back again, even though the Trinity had originally already possessed us once. Both Romans 6:17–22 and 1 Corinthians 6:20 and 7:23 emphasize that we are "bought with a price." Now we have a complete change of masters!

12) My left foot and leg have been crippled for over 15 years because of an original misdiagnosis and a foot rebuilding that led to a broken leg which healed crooked. During all the time since then I've worn a leg brace, but frequently get wounds inside of it. As a result, my right leg is quite strong and able to carry me on crutches, but it also makes a sacrifice when it gets swollen and sore from overuse. This time—with more than four months of strain—it became enormously distended and bruised and has yet to recover fully. Much more extensively, Christ's *sacrifice* on the cross was prefigured by the entire mosaic pattern of blood animal sacrifices. The book of Hebrews proclaims that Jesus'death was effective for forgiveness, particularly because He was both priest and offering—although we don't fully understand how and why His death was the culminating termination of such sacrifice.

13) After dead skin, infection, and a problematic screw were all removed, it was remarkable how fast the surgery wound healed and how quickly the hole from the screw and the broken bones filled in. Truly this recent restoration of my foot has been exceptionally freeing. Far more thoroughly, the *forgiveness* made available to us through Christ's work emancipates us to live differently. We are no longer bogged down in guilt and regrets; we are liberated to begin afresh.

14, 15) One of my biggest problems in this ordeal was that it all seemed so meaningless. There was no explanation for how (or why) I burned my foot in the first place (which led to the series of complications), and it certainly didn't do me—or anyone else—any good. That realization, however, did make me more grateful for the sufferings of Christ. For as Isaiah 53 teaches us, the *Suffering Servant* went like a *lamb to the slaughter*—"wounded for our transgressions, crushed for our iniquities." His suffering makes ours (which now seem so minor) more bearable.

16) One of the worst side effects of this long process with my foot was that I couldn't really exercise or keep the rest of my body or psyche in shape. As a result, my kidney functioning took a severe dip. The situation doesn't look very good as I head (much more quickly than I anticipated) toward needing dialysis or a transplant. My kidneys seem to require a miracle to be saved. And truly it is a complex miracle that through the sufferings and death and resurrection of Christ we have been given the gift of *salvation*. Who can understand it, but we are indeed liberated, rescued, saved through Christ's work!

17, 18, 19) The most important lesson I've learned in all this mess is that I easily turn bodily health into an idol and desire it more than God. What I need more than anything is spiritual healing to move away from myself into closer relationship with God. That is the promise that Galatians 4 gives us: this surprising news that through Christ's work of salvation, we have been *adopted* as God's children. Now we can learn an entirely new vocabulary of life. Now the gifts that we get are *sanctification, eternal life.*

20) This odyssey has deepened my teaching, I pray. I hope that my work for the sake of the world is stronger, even though that is an extremely tiny part of all that God is doing to *renew the cosmos.* St. Athanasius emphasizes that all of this, all God's work, is of a piece:

> *The renewal of creation has been wrought by the Self-same Word Who made it in the beginning.* There is thus no inconsistency between creation and salvation; for the One Father has employed the same Agent for both works, effecting the salvation of the world through the same Word Who made it at first.[71]

Of course, these analogies are pitifully inadequate. We'd have to multiply the personal examples by the skillions (or, for the mathematicians, by a googleplex[googleplex]) to begin to imagine the unfathomed enormity of God's gifts to us in Christ.

And most amazing: we don't deserve any of it at all. What a scandalously prodigal God we have!

RESURRECTION

The resurrection of Christ is so huge in its cosmic implications, that anything we could say about it is horrendously too small. Attempts both to explain it or praise it will always be inadequate. We need our best arts and literature to catch feeble glimpses of the majestic mystery. For example, C. S. Lewis gives a soul-stirring account in his children's story, *The Lion, the Witch, and the Wardrobe.*[72]

Comparably, composer Randall Thompson has written a gorgeous anthem for choirs that uses only the word *Alleluia!* over and over, but the piece increases in volume throughout and ends with full resonance and bright acclamation. Once, my dear friend Thomas Gieschen conducted the Lutheran Choir of Chicago in a performance of this famous piece, but kept the choir at *pianissimo* throughout its entirety. The quietness kept me on the edge of my seat—waiting for him to urge the choir to crescendo. When I asked him about it later, he said something to this effect: "Christ's resurrection is too magnificent. The choir could never get loud or rich enough to express it, so I thought I'd make it obvious that all of our glories are forever an understatement."

A far worse corruption than inadequate adoration of God's work in raising Christ, of course, is to doubt its historicity. Some people think the physical resurrection of Jesus can't be true because of supposed discrepancies between the four Gospel accounts, but as N. T. Wright points out, we twenty-first-century readers should not forget that "In the ancient world, someone who was intending to tell people what actually happened did not feel obliged (any more than a good journalist, or indeed a real practising historian, would today) to mention every single feature of every single incident."[73] In fact, he stresses, if nothing really happened and the story was invented at a later time, then we would expect all the accounts to be the same.

It is not possible in this brief entry to summarize Wright's massive and masterly scholarship, but his enormous research into pagan, First Testament, post-biblical Judaic, New Testament, and early Christian writings establishes the historic Christian conviction that Jesus physically rose from the dead (contrary to the reductionisms of such people as John Dominic Crossan and Marcus Borg) and that His resurrection changed the world forever.

As one example, we can glance briefly at Luke. Wright demonstrates how every detail in Luke contributes in its context to underscore the Gospel's two main points: that in the resurrection "the divine plan for Israel and the world has come to its unexpected climax, and that you are hereby commissioned to implement it in the world" (649).

Most fascinating is how Wright elaborates this by pointing out parallels between the first two and the last chapters of Luke, including angels announcing Jesus as Israel's Messiah (1:32; 2:11, 26; 24:26, 46), Simeon's pronouncement that the infant Jesus would bring salvation for Israel and the Gentiles and Jesus' commissioning (2:32; 24:47), Anna and Cleopas as those looking for redemption (2:38; 24:21), and the contrast between the couple Mary and Joseph, who search for Jesus three days and receive from Him a strange answer about divine necessity, an important theme in Luke (2:49), and Jesus' own words on the same subject in 24:25–26 (see also 24:7, 44) (650–651). In short, "Easter, for Luke is about the meaning of history . . . and the task and shape of the church . . ." (649).

We corrupt the resurrection, then, not only if we deny its historicity, but also if we fail to live its implications now. I'm sure all of us are guilty.

Luke shows throughout his final Gospel chapter and in Acts 1 that Jesus manifested Himself physically alive with many proofs, but he makes that cosmic by the whole Gospel's confrontation with the kingdoms of the world and his decisive conclusion that Jesus is verifiably the world's true Lord

(653). Do we trust those proofs? Do we submit to Him now in everything as our Lord?

We need to keep remembering the verb tenses in the Church's great confession, "Christ has died; Christ *is* risen; Christ will come again!" Is He risen in our lives, too?

ASCENSION

Where on earth did Jesus go? What in heaven's name happened at the ascension? Jesus certainly wasn't just schmooled (that's not a word, but pretend it is—it sounds like what I mean) into God. Yet the ascension is more often ignored, reduced, distorted, or compromised than most of the other words in this book.

Some corruptions of this event arise because contemporary people don't know what the Bible means by the word *heaven*. By misunderstanding "heaven" many reject the ascension completely as the product of an outdated cosmology that pictured a three-tiered universe with heaven above the earth and hell beneath it. Such people gloat that the scientist Copernicus squelched such a silly notion long ago. Some then deduce that the ascension was just a "spiritual" thing—an attitudinal change on the part of the disciples or perhaps their failure to have more visions of a "supposedly resurrected" Christ.

However, as scholar Douglas Farrow demonstrates, such false assumptions about the nature of the ascension and the meaning of the event arose long before the Polish astronomer existed. Farrow clarifies that

> the doctrine of the ascension was contentious in the early church—let us say, in the second to the sixth century— . . . precisely because of a spiritualizing tendency of this sort, first among the Gnostics, then among the followers of Origen. And whence did that tendency arise, if not because a bodily ascension such as Luke describes was *already* incompatible with the cosmology and soteriology of the ancient pagan world?[74]

No, the real problem is not that by Jesus' ascension into heaven Luke is suggesting a two- or three-tiered universe or recording the disciples' illusions. As N. T. Wright concludes after massive study of ancient literature, "the language of 'heaven' and 'earth' . . . was regularly employed in a sophisticated theological manner, to denote the parallel and interlocking universes" inhabited by God (the former) and human beings (the latter). Luke's account does not copy pagan stories, as some scholars assert, because it (quite politically) emphasizes that the kingdom was restored to Israel "by its representative Messiah being enthroned as the world's true Lord."[75]

The problem with which we must wrestle concerning Christ's ascension is not, therefore, an ancient cosmology which placed heaven above the earth; rather the issue is Christ's new resurrection body, which is both physical and "transphysical" (Wright's term for what the earliest traditions recognized and Paul later theologized and named with words like *incorruptible*).[76] In this sense, the ascension is not about going up, but about moving from one universe to another, interlocking one.

The ascension is a *pivotal* event in the history of God's actions on the world's behalf and for our understanding of what it means to be the Church. It is referred to directly at least 35 times in the Bible (and many other times indirectly).[77] Though Christians today ignore it, the early Christians made it an essential part of their summaries of the faith, as in 1 Timothy 3:16:

> He was revealed in flesh,
>   vindicated in spirit,
>   seen by angels,
>   proclaimed among Gentiles,
>   believed in throughout the world,
>   taken up in glory.

In contrast, then, to various spiritualizers or non-observers, we must begin by understanding that the ascension was, as Farrow emphasizes, a real departure, the exchanging of a shared—though no longer [since the resurrection] a fully common—history for an altogether distinct and unique one. That this departure and exchange took place in the form of a dramatic gesture is plain enough; space travel was never in view. But it did take place. . . . [I]t was the act in which the link between our fallen world and the new creation was fully forged. Moreover, it was the act in which the problem of the presence and the absence came into being, the problem that defines the eschatological situation and necessitates the peculiar sacramental form of the people of God.[78]

It is crucial that we perceive what exactly is at stake in the ascension. It must have a "genuine this-worldly component," a precise historical manifestation and not be some sort of purely abstract transcendence, for, if the latter were the case, then Christ would be "indeed atopic and atemporal," and His "personal human identity" would be "beclouded" in His ascension. Put another way, if the movement of the ascension were primarily *beyond* "our corrupted space and time" rather than *within* it, then what do the Church's sacraments mean and what is the difference between the Church and the world (39)? Christians believe that in the human elements of the sacraments (water, bread, wine) we receive the presence of Christ. The Bible also insists that Christ is present in the midst of His people. That is why the real issue of the ascension is that Jesus is both absent and present since that event.

So what do we actually *know* about this mystery of the ascension? We know *where* Jesus went, for He told us that He was going to the Father, from whom He had come (John 16:5–11). We know *why* He went: to prepare a place for us with His Father, to which He will bring us (John 14:2–3). We know that He is the Way *because* He went (John 13:31–14:31; 20:17). *How* He went is through the entire route of the incarnation, culminating in the cross and the resurrection. "And the *consequence* of his going is a mission of the Spirit aimed at the proclamation of the Father's open house" (36).

Because Jesus ascended, Christians live in a unique place in the world—a place of both "eager expectation" and "groaning." In this place we are called courageously to "refuse either to become irrelevant to the world or to be in conformity with it. Withdrawal and worldliness are alike repugnant to a eucharistic worldview" (73). This will cost us—even to the point of death—if we really love our neighbors with all the fullness of Christ's radical love.

Karl Barth was an important theologian of the ascension, because he recognized that the time between it and the resurrection was not merely a period of subjective, "spiritual" experiences for the disciples. Instead, Farrow summarizes, "It was a new coming of Jesus himself with his humanity intact and his divinity no longer veiled. It was the time in which God was clearly seen and known to live as this man, and this man as God." The ascension ended that time—setting "definite limit to it, preserving its particularity"—but it didn't negate His presence. Rather, His presence is now "hidden with God. . . . And by fixing [all His time, His life and death and resurrection] with God, it fixed it at the heart of every time" (235).

Therefore (and this is an incomprehensibly immense and unfathomed *therefore*), we Christians live in the tension of Jesus' presence and absence. Since reading Farrow's book, I have felt a deeply stirring elation in my life because of the implicit call and goal in that tension. We are Christ's people, His Body in fact, and He has commissioned us to do His work until He comes again. By the power of the Spirit poured out at Pentecost, we are equipped to live in this meanwhile time—knowing that He will come again to take us across the present division between God's eternity and our time, believing that He is present with us in the sacraments, but in His absence fulfilling the mission He gave us by the power of the Spirit He also gave us.

The Christian community lives as "the prophetic sign to the world" that at the ascension God enthroned Jesus at His right hand, at the center of all existence throughout space and time (32). Someday we will see that for ourselves. In the meanwhile, the ascension gives us double vision: we see the reality of the world around us; we know the truth of Christ's cosmic presence. We longingly look for the day when He will come again, and the latter will swallow up the former!

PENTECOST

Yesterday it was my immense delight to preach as a guest on Pentecost Sunday. The enjoyment was multiplied because the host pastor (a good friend who presided when my husband and I married) did not know I was coming. He had planned a 40th anniversary surprise celebration for his wife, but the congregation flabbergasted them both by flying me there without their knowing. My exhilaration in being part of the secret—and disclosing it only when, as the congregation waited, I walked out of hiding to proclaim the Gospel lesson and preach—suggested to me the Father's immense pleasure in pouring out the awaited but unexpected Spirit on Christ's astonished disciples on the first Pentecost.

We need to be somewhat shocked as we celebrate Pentecost each year, for certainly God's extravagant gifting is more than we can absorb. A few of the festivities that have astounded me most were a musician who rumbled the 32' organ pipes to suggest the wind of the Spirit; a texture artist who cut out scores of bright orange and red thick and shiny plastic flame shapes and suspended them from the church sanctuary ceiling on a gigantic mobile that ceaselessly soared and caught the lights and flashed them in brilliant shimmerings; and a senior citizen who joined the people reading the first Pentecost crowd's words in French, Spanish, German, Polish, and Norwegian and spoke his line in Lakota.

These were extraordinary experiences, but, of course, not at all big enough to catch the actual dramatic change of Pentecost. As C. S. Lewis imagines, "God became man to turn creatures into sons: not simply to produce better men of the old kind but to produce a new kind of man. It is not like teaching a horse to jump better and better but like turning a horse into a winged creature."[79]

Far more dangerous than making our Pentecost celebrations too ordinary is the corruption of reducing the work of the Holy Spirit to only dramatic incidents, like that first Pentecost. Then we lose what really happened that day: the Church was born. Lives, in all their dailiness, were radically transformed. The Church thereafter—with no canon of Scriptures, no creeds, no hierarchy—flourished because the apostles and their new converts simply relied on that same Spirit power to lead and guide the Church in both the mundane and the extraordinary.[80]

We have lost that reliance.

We have also lost the trust that the Spirit works in quiet little ways in daily life. For example, as detailed in the segment on the scandal of the cross, this year my foot broke as soon as I began walking after a severe burn on my foot finally healed. To my great surprise, the necessary surgery to remove a screw and the following weeks of trying to let the heel bone heal without letting the bones deteriorate further were not horribly devastating to me, though I had been eagerly anticipating walking and swimming again for several months. I wasn't exactly giddy with delight, of course, at the prospect of facing a longer period of non-walking, but the Holy Spirit held me in check, kept me from too many dips into depression, reminded me of countless reasons for gratitude, empowered my speaking meanwhile. I even enjoyed serving as cantor and offertory soloist for worship the day before surgery because praising God was the most important thing I could do to prepare for the upcoming weeks of further health frustrations. Because I know my own personality amid high levels of strain and because not walking has been so inconvenient in my work, the question is insistent: could this relative equilibrium have been anything but the work of the Holy Spirit?

In large ways, in small ways, since that memorable pouring out of grace on Jesus' community on one day in history, the presence of the Holy Spirit keeps changing everything. In the absence of Jesus, the Holy Spirit equips us to do His work as

His Body until He comes again and brings God's kingdom to its culmination to the glory of the Father.

We are not just trying to jump higher as we seek to do God's will in our personal lives and as a Christian community. We are airborne!

PAROUSIA
(CHRIST'S SECOND COMING)

"Do you really believe that silly stuff about Jesus coming to get you and taking you to heaven where the streets are all gold and such?" my self-avowed "militant atheist" student challenged me one day in my office at the university where I taught Literature of the Bible. Equally glibly I answered that day long ago that I truly knew that at the end of time I would be with Christ and that there, in God's presence, everything would be turned upside down. Here we think gold is of utmost importance, but there we will just walk on the stuff.

Recently I've thought much more urgently about the *parousia*, the coming of Jesus at the end of time—partly because so many people think it is just a silly notion and partly because His coming is so corrupted on the opposite side by those who try to calendarize it or write best selling books about all the events that will precede it. Those books betray appalling misreadings of the Scriptures[81] and propel mistakenly apocalyptic politics and policies.

But the *parousia* is corrupted in less ghastly, but nonetheless weighty ways by churches who pray, "Come, Lord Jesus," and yet make 5- or 15-year plans. Why do we Christians do that? Why do we rely on programs and business models to chart our future or organize our meanwhile life instead of letting the Spirit guide us daily as we *be* Christ's Body for the sake of the world?

Don't get me wrong. I realize that at times there is a necessity for making plans, gathering money, building a facility, arranging meetings, and so forth for the sake of doing ministry.

My point is simply that we seem too parked in this world.

Don't get me wrong again. I don't mean that we Christians should be so "heavenly minded that we're no earthly good." It just seems that we're often so earthly minded that we can't do any heavenly good.

This is a somewhat similar problem to that which Paul addresses when the Corinthian Christians were failing to engage in genuine ministry, fighting about all the wrong things, siding with factions, living in jealousy instead of working together and each contributing their gifts for *eternal* work that would not be burned up like straw (1 Cor. 3:1–15).

How do we understand our true ministry and that of our churches these days? We get too involved in taking care of buildings or running programs, fighting over worship or handling all the administrivia, and seem to have no urgency about *being little Christs*, as Martin Luther would say, for the sake of our neighbors. We find it too hard to live that way, in the tension of being Christ's Body, doing His mission, in this time of absence between His ascension and parousia. We find it too precarious to live in moment by moment dependence upon the Spirit which He gave us to know His presence. We want to be in control and direct our own futures. And we're too comfortable or too proud of our own accomplishments to want Him really to come again!

It seems that churches make 15-year plans because the congregation members need some sort of spark plug to get them going in ministry, some sort of vision toward which to move. But don't we have a much more powerful lighter in the cross and resurrection of Jesus Christ?—for that is the beginning we had in our baptisms, when we died to ourselves and rose with Him into the new creation. And don't we have a much more combustible kindling in the ascension, which ignited us into the mission of carrying Christ's presence throughout the world? And look at the wind we received at Pentecost, when the Spirit's breath blasted us into boldness! And won't that current continue to fan our flames as we await with fiery ardor the culmination of the Trinity's work at the end of time? Isn't the vision of the glowing kingdom of righteousness and justice, truth and peace a sufficient flare to guide our ways in love until the day when the absence of Jesus is no more and His presence is no longer veiled?

How does that fire of the Triune God work in and through the blazing passion of your Christian community and your own particular life? As God burns away our corruptions of language so that we can be more precisely faithful and thoroughly gracious in talking the walk, how is the Trinity informing us to walk the talk?

NOTES

Introduction

1. Alan Jacobs quotes C. S. Lewis, who declared in the preface of his first book on Christian apologetics, "I have believed myself to be re-stating ancient and orthodox doctrines. If any parts of the book are 'original,' in the sense of being novel or unorthodox, they are so against my will and as a result of my ignorance."

Lewis contends that this "plain, central' Christian faith, when examined closely and historically, "turns out to be no insipid interdenominational transparency, but something positive, self-consistent, and inexhaustible. Because it is positive, it provides direction for the spiritual inquirer; because it is self-consistent, it provides security; because it is inexhaustible, it provides delight." Alan Jacobs, *Vanity Fair: Moral Essays on the Present Age* (Grand Rapids: Brazos Press, 2001), 121–124.

2. Kenneth L. Woodward [Religion Editor of *Newsweek*], "Reply to Andrew Lang" [staff writer in the Office of Communication in the United Church of Christ who objected to Woodward's review of the new UCC hymnbook], *How Shall We Sing the Lord's Song: An Assessment of The New Century Hymnal*, ed. Richard L. Christensen (Centerville, MA: Confessing Christ, 1997), 54.

3. T. R. Reid, *Confucius Lives Next Door: What Living in the East Teaches Us About Living in the West* (New York: Random House, 1995), 102.

4. Reid, *Confucius Lives Next Door*, 103–104.

5. This idea comes from Jacques Ellul, *The Humiliation of the Word*, trans. Joyce Main Hanks (Grand Rapids: Eerdmans, 1985).

6. Richard B. Hays, "Reading Scripture in Light of the Resurrection," *The Art of Reading Scripture*, eds. Ellen F. Davis and Richard B. Hays (Grand Rapids: Eerdmans, 2003), 220.

205

7. Joseph Sittler, *Gravity and Grace* (Minneapolis: Augsburg, 1986), as quoted in *For All the Saints: A Prayer Book For and By the Church*, Vol. I: Year 1: Advent to the Day of Pentecost, compiled and edited by Frederick J. Schumacher with Dorothy A. Zelenko (Delhi, NY: American Lutheran Publicity Bureau, 1994), 954–955.

8. See John Howard Yoder, *Preface to Theology: Christology and Theological Method* (Grand Rapids: Brazos Press, 2002), 176–179.

Part I: God

1. See Luke Timothy Johnson, *The Real Jesus: The Misguided Quest for the Historical Jesus and the Truth of the Traditional Gospels*, paperback edition (San Francisco: HarperSanFrancisco, 1997).

2. See Tom Wright, *The Original Jesus: The Life and Vision of a Revolutionary* (Grand Rapids: Eerdmans, 1996).

3. I'm grateful to Kati Kovacs, former Regent College student, for teaching me these pronouns.

4. William C. Placher, *Jesus the Savior: The Meaning of Jesus Christ for Christian Faith* (Louisville: Westminster John Knox, 2001), 44–45.

5. See John Howard Yoder, *The Politics of Jesus*, 2nd ed. (Grand Rapids: Eerdmans, 1994), 162–192.

6. Christopher A. Hall, *Learning Theology with the Church Fathers* (Downers Grove, IL: InterVarsity Press, 2002), 218.

7. See Marva J. Dawn, *Powers, Weakness, and the Tabernacling of God* (Grand Rapids: Eerdmans, 2001).

8. See Marva J. Dawn, "Introduction to the Gospel of John," *Renovaré Spiritual Formation Study Bible*, Richard J. Foster, ed. (San Francisco: HarperSanFrancisco, forthcoming).

9. Placher, *Jesus the Savior*, 49.

10. Placher refers to David S. Yeago, "Jesus of Nazareth and Cosmic Redemption: The Relevance of St. Maximus the Confessor," *Modern Theology* 12 (1996): 167.

11. Placher, *Jesus the Savior*, 49.

12. This is the formal confession of faith set out by the Council of Chalcedon, translated in J. N. D. Kelly, *Early Christian Doctrines*, 2nd ed. (New York: Harper & Row, 1960), 339–340.

13. Gregory of Nazianzus, *The Third Theological Oration—On the Son* in *Christology of the Later Fathers*, ed. Edward R. Hardy (Philadelphia: Westminster, 1954), 174–175.

14. Rowan Williams, *The Dwelling of the Light: Praying with Icons of Christ* (Grand Rapids: Eerdmans, 2003), 6–7.

15. For an imaginative suggestion of the kind of conversations Mary might have had with her son, see Walter Wangerin, Jr., *Mary's First Christmas*, illus. Timothy Ladwig (Grand Rapids: Zondervan, 1998). See also David G. Benner, *The Gift of Being Yourself: The Sacred Call to Self Discovery* (Downers Grove, IL: InterVarsity Press, 2004), 93–94.

16. Yoder, *Preface to Theology*, 140 (emphasis mine).

17. For an insightful comparison of Jesus-as-God in Mark's Gospel and Emperor Nero's triumphant procession as an attempt to be considered divine, see "the man who would be god," chapter 3 in Thomas Schmidt's *A Scandalous Beauty: The Artistry of God and the Way of the Cross* (Grand Rapids: Brazos Press, 2002), 31–37.

18. Robert L. Wilken, *Remembering the Christian Past* (Grand Rapids: Eerdmans, 1995), 87.

19. Wilken, *Remembering the Christian Past*, 88, citing Gregory of Nyssa, *Contra Eunomium* 1:158. See also Christopher Hall's discussion of Athanasius' comments in *Four Discourses Against the Arians* over these names in *Learning Theology with the Church Fathers*, 47–51.

20. On the incipient Trinitarianism in the Bible, particularly in the Gospel of Matthew, see R. W. L. Moberly, *The Bible, Theology, and Faith: A Study of Abraham and Jesus* (Cambridge: Cambridge University Press, 2000).

21. Allen Vander Pol, *God in Three Persons: Biblical Testimony to the Trinity* (Phillipsburg, NJ: Presbyterian and Reformed, 2001).

22. J. N. D. Kelly, *Early Christian Creeds*, 3rd ed. (London: Longman, 1972), 23. Catherine Mowry LaCugna agrees with this statement, but thinks Kelly overstates his case when he thereby concludes, "The impression inevitably conveyed is that the conception of the threefold manifestation of the Godhead was embedded deeply in Christian thinking from the start." See Catherine Mowry LaCugna, *God for Us: The Trinity and Christian Life* (San Francisco: Harper-SanFrancisco, 1991), 129. Indeed, Kelly uses anachronistic language ("threefold manifestation," "Godhead") in that sentence, but his point seems justified. My quick skimming of the New Testament recently disclosed all these texts which mention the three persons of the Trinity with a sense of equality and mutuality: Matt. 3:16–17; 28:19; Mark 1:10–11; Luke 1:35; 3:21–22; 10:21; John 1:32–33; 3:34; 14:16–17, 26; 15:26; 16:13–15; Acts 2:32–33, 38–39; 5:31–32; 7:55; 10:38; 20:21–23, 28; Rom. 5:5–6; 8:9, 11; 14:17–18; 15:16, 19, 30; 1 Cor. 6:11; 12:3–6;

2 Cor. 1:21–22; 3:3; 13:13; Gal. 4:6; Eph. 1:3–14; 2:13–18; 3:14–17; 4:4–6; Phil. 3:3; 2 Thess. 2:13; Heb. 10:29; 1 Peter 1:2; 4:14; 1 John 4:2, 13–14. Since the day of that rapid overview, I have found several more passages in my morning devotional reading.

23. Wilken, *Remembering the Christian Past*, 76. Page references to this book in the following paragraphs will be given parenthetically in the text.

24. Karl Rahner, *The Trinity* (New York: Herder & Herder, 1970), 10–11.

25. Wilken, *Remembering*, 81. On the cruciality of recognizing God as Trinity at the heart of reality, see also Stanley Hauerwas, *With the Grain of the Universe: The Church's Witness and Natural Theology* (Grand Rapids: Brazos Press, 2001).

26. LaCugna, *God for Us*, 2. Page references to this book in the following paragraphs will be given parenthetically in the text.

27. Roger E. Olson and Christopher A. Hall, *The Trinity* (Grand Rapids: Eerdmans, 2002), 1.

28. Henri Nouwen, *Sabbatical Journey*, 134, as quoted in *The Heart of Henri Nouwen: His Words of Blessing*, eds. Rebecca Laird and Michael J. Christensen (New York: Crossroad, 2003), 147.

29. Dante Alighiere (1268–1321), *The Divine Comedy*, Canto XXIV, trans. H.R. Huse (New York: Holt, Rinehart & Winston, 1961), quoted in *For All the Saints*, 166.

30. The numbers *11* and over *170* are given in Wilken, *Remembering the Christian Past*, 89.

31. Gregory of Nazianzus, *The Third Theological Oration—On the Son*, ed. Edward R. Hardy, *Christology of the Later Fathers*, 171, as cited in Hall, *Learning Theology with the Church Fathers*, 64.

32. Charles Michael Jacobs (1875–1938), *Helps On the Road*, from J.W. Doberstein, *Minister's Prayer Book* (Philadelphia: Muhlenberg Press, 1958), as quoted in *For All the Saints: A Prayer Book For and By the Church*, Vol. II, Year 1: The Season After Pentecost, compiled and edited by Frederick J. Schumacher with Dorothy A. Zelenko (Delhi, NY: American Lutheran Publicity Bureau, 1995), 484.

33. Basil the Great, *On the Holy Spirit*, trans. David Anderson (Crestwood, NY: St. Vladimir's Seminary Press, 1980), 76, as cited in Hall, *Learning Theology with the Church Fathers*, 117.

34. See my plea to stop dividing churches and their worship by means of the ill-defined words *contemporary* and *traditional* in chapter 15, "Worship Is Not a Matter of Taste," in Marva J. Dawn, *A Royal "Waste" of Time: The Splendor of Worshiping God and Being Church for the World* (Grand Rapids: Eerdmans, 1999), 186–193.

35. Ellul, *The Humiliation of the Word*.

36. Kenda Creasy Dean and Ron Foster claim in *The Godbearing Life: The Art of Soul Tending for Youth Ministry* (Nashville: Upper Room, 1998) that young people, in an age of mind-boggling special effects, need a God whose transcendence is the real thing. See also Robert Wuthnow's *After Heaven: Spirituality in America since the 1950s* (Berkeley: University of California Press, 1998) and Kenda Creasy Dean, *Practicing Passion: Youth and the Quest for a Passionate Church* (Grand Rapids: Eerdmans, 2004).

Part II: Why Do Human Beings and the World Need God?

1. See Cornelius Plantinga, Jr., *Not the Way It's Supposed to Be: A Breviary of Sin* (Grand Rapids: Eerdmans,1995), x.

2. *Lutheran Book of Worship* (Minneapolis: Augsburg, 1978), 56.

3. The same could be said for all victims of occupational forces, but the Palestinian crisis has lasted for well over fifty years and is often overlooked (or even abetted) by Christians. See the moving account by Lutheran pastor in Bethlehem Mitri Raheb in *Bethlehem Besieged: Stories of Hope in Times of Trouble* (Minneapolis: Fortress Press, 2004).

4. In my writing I always capitalize the word *Joy* because I do not mean a simple exuberance, happiness, pleasure, or excitement caused by circumstances. I use the word to signify that deep, abiding confidence, gratitude, and trust that are ours when our lives are transformed by the truths of our meta-narrative—especially by the fact that eternity has broken into the present because of the Resurrection and we live now in the Joy of God's future kingdom in all its fullness.

5. The suggestion that wanting to have the knowledge of good and evil is an intolerance of mystery is from Charlie Peacock, *New Way to Be Human: A Provocative Look at What It Means to Follow Jesus* (Colorado Springs: Shaw, 2004), 39.

6. Much of what follows is due to Dietrich Bonhoeffer, *Creation and Fall: A Theological Interpretation of Genesis 1–3*, trans. John C. Fletcher, revised by editorial staff of SCM Press (New York: Macmillan, 1959; originally published in 1937), 64–65. No doubt influenced by the world around him shortly after Hitler's Nazi party had seized control of Germany, Bonhoeffer delivered these lectures on Genesis 1–3 at the University of Berlin.

7. A lovely lesson about dependence is given at the beginning of one of George MacDonald's children's stories. The storyteller

declares, "'The sheep are not very knowing creatures, so they are something better instead. They are wise—that is, they are obedient—creatures, obedience being the very best wisdom. For, they have a shepherd to take care of them, who knows where to take them, especially when a storm comes on." George MacDonald, "A Scot's Christmas Story," *The Christmas Stories of George MacDonald* (Elgin, IL: David C. Cook, 1981), 42.

8. Bonhoeffer describes the human condition in a chapter called "The Middle of the Earth." I wonder: is this where J. R. R. Tolkien got the idea for his name *Middle Earth* for the region in which the hobbits and others have to make their choices for good or evil and battle sundry corruptions of power? See J. R. R. Tolkien, Part One: *The Fellowship of the Ring*, Part Two: *The Two Towers*, and Part Three: *The Return of the King* of *The Lord of the Rings* (Boston: Houghton Mifflin, 1955).

9. Bonhoeffer, *Creation and Fall*, 76.

10. Garry Wills, *Reagan's America: Innocents at Home* (Garden City, NY: Doubleday, 1987), 384, as cited in Plantinga, *Not the Way It's Supposed to Be*, 198.

11. David G. Benner, *The Gift of Being Yourself: The Sacred Call to Self Discovery* (Downers Grove, IL: InterVarsity Press, 2004), 63.

12. Christopher A. Hall, *Learning Theology with the Church Fathers* (Downers Grove, IL: InterVarsity Press, 2002), 122–156.

13. N. T. Wright notes the interesting twist, evidenced in George Steiner's book *Errata*, that postmodernism seems to be bringing back the doctrine of original sin in its diatribes against the arrogance of modernism. See the interview with Wright, "Resurrection faith," *Christian Century* 119, no. 26 (Dec. 18–31, 2002), 31.

14. See David Gushee's chapter 19, "Race," in Glen M. Stassen and David P. Gushee, *Christian Ethics as Following Jesus* (Downers Grove, IL: InterVarsity Press, 2003) and Andrew Hacker, *Two Nations: Black and White, Separate, Hostile, Unequal* (New York: Ballantine, 1992).

15. For an excellent, grace-filled discussion that helps us move out of class guilt, see Arthur Simon's *How Much Is Enough?* (Grand Rapids: Baker, 2003). See also Marva J. Dawn, *Unfettered Hope: A Call to Faithful Living in an Affluent Society* (Louisville: Westminster John Knox, 2003).

16. Ps. 106:15–16 as cited in *For All the Saints: A Prayer Book For and By the Church*, Vol. I; Year 1: Advent to the Day of Pentecost, compiled and edited by Frederick J. Schumacher with Dorothy A. Zelenko (Delhi, NY: American Lutheran Publishing Bureau, 1994), 674.

17. Oswald Chambers, "The Relinquished Life," from *My Utmost for His Highest* (Grand Rapids: Discovery House, originally 1935), as cited in *Bread and Wine: Readings for Lent and Easter* (Farmington, PA: Plough, 2003), 34–35, and in "The Offense of the Natural," *My Utmost for His Highest Journal: Selections for the Year* (Uhrichsville, OH: Barbour, nd), December 9.

18. Karl B arth, quoted in Thomas G. Long, "A Response to Douglas John Hall," *Journal for Preachers* 25, no. 1 (Advent, 2001): 16.

19. Long, "A Response to Douglas John Hall," 15.

20. J. K. Rowling, *Harry Potter and the Order of the Phoenix* (New York: Scholastic/Arthur A. Levine, 2003), 223.

21. See C. S. Lewis, *The Screwtape Letters* (New York: Macmillan, 1941).

22. Peacock, *New Way to Be Human*, 38.

23. Arthur Piepkorn (1907–1973), *Response*, Vol. 5, no. 2 (Lutheran Society for Worship, Music & the Arts, 1963), 73, as quoted in *For All the Saints*, 481–482.

24. One of the best books on the principalities is Jacques Ellul, *Money and Power*, trans. LaVonne Neff (Downers Grove, IL: InterVarsity Press, 1984). See also Marva J. Dawn, *Powers, Weakness, and the Tabernacling of God* (Grand Rapids: Eerdmans, 2001) and "The Concept of 'the Principalities and Powers' in the Works of Jacques Ellul," Ph.D. diss., University of Notre Dame, 1992 (Ann Arbor, MI: University Microfilms, #9220614). Other descriptions are offered in *Is It a Lost Cause? Having the Heart of God for the Church's Children* (Grand Rapids: Eerdmans, 1997) and in chapter 5 of Marva J. Dawn and Eugene H. Peterson, *The Unnecessary Pastor: Rediscovering the Call* (Grand Rapids: Eerdmans, 1999).

25. "A Prophetic Epistle from United Methodists Calling Our Brother George W. Bush to Repent," *Christian Century* 120, no. 7 (April 5, 2003): 28.

26. Cited in David McCullough, *Brave Companions: Portraits in History* (New York: Simon & Schuster/Touchstone, 1992), 227.

27. C. S. Lewis, *The Great Divorce* (New York: Macmillan, 1945).

28. Many lovely examples of saints who have known God's presence in the stage of death are given in the final section of stories in *Soul Searchers: An Anthology of Spiritual Journeys*, compiled by Teresa de Bertodano (Grand Rapids: Eerdmans, 2001).

29. John Chrysostom (344–407), *Catechatical Address*, quoted in *For All the Saints*, 980–981.

Part III: Actions of God

1. Philip Yancey, *Soul Survivor: How My Faith Survived the Church* (London: Hodder & Stoughton, 2001), 241.

2. I'm thinking of such Dorothy Sayers works as *Have His Carcase: A Lord Peter Wimsey Mystery* (New York: HarperPaperbacks, 1995; first published 1932) or *Busman's Honeymoon* (New York: Harper-Paperbacks, 1995; first published 1937), both Lord Peter Wimsey and Harriet Vane mysteries. Though not technically a mystery novel, G. K. Chesterton's *The Man Who Was Thursday: A Nightmare* (New York: Dodd, Mead & Company, 1908), has a perfect mixture of clues, suspense, humor, moral lessons (though not didactic), and wonder.

3. John Howard Yoder, *Preface to Theology: Christology and Theological Method* (Grand Rapids: Brazos Press, 2002), 58.

4. Miroslav Volf, "Faith Matters: Married Love," *Christian Century* 119, no. 12 (June 5–12, 2002): 35.

5. See Matt. 13:35; 25:34; John 17:24; Eph. 1:4; 1 Peter 1:20; and Rev. 13:8.

6. Søren Kierkegaard (1813–1855), as quoted in *For All the Saints: A Prayer Book For and By the Church*, Vol. I; Year 1: Advent to the Day of Pentecost, compiled and edited by Frederick J. Schumacher with Dorothy A. Zelenko (Delhi, NY: American Lutheran Publicity Bureau, 1994), 834.

7. No one describes this better than Dr. Paul Brand, who tried to invent pain devices for lepers so that their limbs wouldn't be destroyed by injuries not felt. Invariably the patients shut the devices off rather than willingly experience pain—and thereby they lost the alarm that would alert them to danger. See Paul W. Brand and Philip Yancey, *The Gift of Pain: Why We Hurt and What We Can Do About It* (Grand Rapids: Zondervan, 1997).

8. Introductory Essay by Sharon Begley, *The Hand of God: Thoughts and Images Reflecting the Spirit of the Universe*, ed. Michael Reagan (Kansas City, MO: Andrews McMeel Universal Company, 1999), 9.

9. C. S. Lewis, *The Magician's Nephew* (New York: HarperTrophy, 1955), 126–127. See the whole creation account on 116–135.

10. This movement began with Genesis 22 when the LORD shows Himself to be a different God from the rest by not asking for child sacrifice. See John H. Yoder, "If Abraham Is Our Father," *The Original Revolution* (Scottdale, PA: Herald Press, 1972), 85–104.

11. This summary of the nature of God's wrath is derived from Dr. Terence E. Fretheim's presentation, "Reflections on The Wrath

of God in the Old Testament," at the American Academy of Religion/ Society of Biblical Literature annual meeting in Denver on November 18, 2001. His paper is abbreviated in *Horizons in Biblical Theology* 24 (2002). A more complete description of his main points can be found in chapter 5 of Marva J. Dawn, *Unfettered Hope: A Call to Faithful Living in an Affluent Society* (Louisville: Westminster John Knox, 2003), 118–122.

12. Yoder, *Preface to Theology*, 168. Page references to this book in the following paragraphs will be given parenthetically in the text.

13. See chapter eight, "Innocent Notes on 'The Hermeneutic Question,'" in *Sources and Trajectories: Eight Early Articles by Jacques Ellul that Set the Stage*, translated and edited by Marva J. Dawn (Grand Rapids: Eerdmans, 1997), 184–203.

14. Other scholars offer helpful approaches. In a Notre Dame course, redaction criticism scholar Jerome Murphy-O'Connor insisted that Matthew's rendering of the Hebrew word for "young woman" in Isaiah 7:14 with the Greek word *parthenos* or "virgin" would make no redactional sense unless it was based on some historical conviction. Raymond Brown discusses that conviction in terms of Matthew's and Luke's handling of a "pre-Gospel narrative of the annunciation of the Davidic Messiah's birth from a virgin through the creative power of the Holy Spirit" (Raymond E. Brown, *The Birth of the Messiah: A Commentary on the Infancy Narratives in Matthew and Luke* [New York: Doubleday, 1977], 161).

15. Martin Luther, "The Magnificat" (1521), *American Edition of Luther's Works*, Vol. 21 (St. Louis: Concordia, 1956), as quoted in *For All the Saints: A Prayer Book For and By the Church*, Vol. IV; Year 2: The Season After Pentecost, compiled and edited by Frederick J. Schumacher with Dorothy A. Zelenko (Delhi, NY: American Lutheran Publicity Bureau, 1996), 1307.

16. The best book I've ever seen on the death of God in Christ is Alan E. Lewis, *Between Cross and Resurrection: A Theology of Holy Saturday* (Grand Rapids: Eerdmans, 2001).

17. St. Athanasius, *On the Incarnation (De Incarnatione Verbi Dei)*, trans. Sister Penelope Lawson, C.S.M.V. (New York: Macmillan, 1946), 13. Page references to this book in the following paragraphs will be given parenthetically in the text. I am forever thankful to Professor Charles Kannengeiser, who demanded in a systematics course at Notre Dame that we repeatedly read this treatise by Athanasius.

18. Dorothy Sayers (1893–1957), *Creed or Chaos?* (A. Wattsins, Inc.; Harcourt Brace 1st American Edition, 1949), as quoted in *For*

All the Saints: A Prayer Book For and By the Church, Vol. III; Year 2: Advent to the Day of Pentecost, compiled and edited by Frederick J. Schumacher with Dorothy A. Zelenko (Delhi, NY: American Lutheran Publicity Bureau, 1995), 156.

19. Lewis, *Between Cross and Resurrection*, 119, emphasis mine.

20. Among the many ways that non-believers like to debunk Christianity that G. K. Chesterton illustrates in his clever Father Brown mysteries, one of the most whimsical is the sham "miracle" in "The Resurrection of Father Brown." See (and enjoy the wit and wisdom of) G. K. Chesterton, *The Complete Father Brown: The Enthralling Adventures of Fiction's Best-Loved Amateur Sleuth*—a subtitle I'm sure Chesterton would never have written for the same reason that Father Brown foiled the sham by refusing to accept fame—(New York: Penguin, 1981), 319–322.

21. According to Littlewood's Law of Miracles posited by a famous mathematician we can look forward to about one miracle a month—if we each experience about 30,000 different events each day and if miracles characterize one out of every million. But questions remain: "What exactly is a miracle? Do they happen merely by chance? Do we even notice them?" *New York Review of Books*, March 25, 2004, as cited in "Century Marks," *Christian Century* 121, no. 7 (April 6, 2004): 7. Reading about Littlewood's Law reminds me of my experience of encountering in Hong Kong the man who had translated my lectures into Chinese the previous week again at the dock for a ferry he never rode except that night to meet his wife on her birthday. Officials estimate that a million people ride the Hong Kong ferries each day.

22. Tom Hanculak, "The Dream That Saved Me," *Notre Dame Magazine* 31, no. 4 (Winter 2002–2003): 42.

23. Interview with N. T. Wright, "Resurrection faith," *Christian Century* 119, no. 26 (Dec. 18–31, 2002): 28.

24. C. S. Lewis, *Mere Christianity* (New York: HarperCollins, 1952).

25. See Lewis, *Between Cross and Resurrection*, 133–162. See also Jürgen Moltmann, *The Crucified God*, trans. R. A. Wilson and J. Bowden (London: SCM and New York: Harper & Row, 1974).

26. See, for example, Terence E. Fretheim, *The Suffering of God: An Old Testament Perspective*, Overtures to Biblical Theology, eds. Walter Brueggemann and John R. Donahue (Philadelphia: Fortress Press, 1984) and Kazoh Kitamori, *Theology of the Pain of God* (Richmond, VA: John Knox, 1958).

27. Lewis, *Between Cross and Resurrection*.

28. For an excellent discussion of the importance of a "theology of the cross" in light of feminist concerns for those who suffer, see Deanna A. Thompson, *Crossing the Divide: Luther, Feminism, and the Cross* (Minneapolis: Fortress Press, 2004).

29. Chesterton, *The Man Who Was Thursday*, 190–191.

30. See the excellent discussion of the artistic and theological merits and failures of Mel Gibson's controversial movie *The Passion of the Christ* in the collection of articles, "The Problem with *The Passion*," *Christian Century* 121, no. 6 (March 23, 2004): 18–23; and Jean Bethke Elshtain, "Faith Matters: Anti-Semitism or anti-Judaism?" *Christian Century* 121, no. 10 (May 18, 2004): 39.

31. See Mark Douglas, *"The Passion of the Christ*: A Review (or why liberals are right for the wrong reasons and conservatives are wrong for the right ones)," *Journal for Preachers* XXVII, no. 4 (Pentecost, 2002): 47–56, and responses by Kathleen M. O'Connor and Iwar Russell-Jones, 57–68.

32. See, for example, the many-dimensioned discussion of the applicability of Girard's work for biblical interpretation in Willard M. Swartley, ed., *Violence Renounced: René Girard, Biblical Studies, and Peacemaking* (Telford, PA: Pandora Press, 2001).

33. Rebecca Parker writes, "No one was saved by the execution of Jesus," in "The Unblessed Child: Rebecca's Story," *Proverbs of Ashes: Violence, Redemptive Suffering, and the Search for What Saves Us* (Boston: Beacon Press, 2001), 211.

34. See John H. Yoder, *The Politics of Jesus*, 2nd ed. (Grand Rapids: Eerdmans, 1994), 162–192.

35. As one example of an artistic response to one Gospel, see Walter Wangerin Jr., *Reliving the Passion: Meditations on the Suffering, Death, and Resurrection of Jesus as Recorded in Mark* (Grand Rapids: Zondervan, 1992).

36. See, for example, Martin Luther, *The 1529 Holy Week and Easter Sermons of Dr. Martin Luther*, Irving L. Sandberg, trans., and Timothy J. Wengert, annotater (St. Louis: Concordia, 1999) or Fleming Rutledge, *The Undoing of Death: Sermons for Holy Week and Easter* (Grand Rapids: Eerdmans, 2002).

37. See the discussion of a few elements of Bach's work in Dawn, *Unfettered Hope*, 131–135.

38. Henri J. M. Nouwen, *In the Name of Jesus: Reflections on Christian Leadership* (New York: Crossroad, 1989).

39. C. S. Lewis, *The Lion, the Witch, and the Wardrobe* (New York: HarperCollins, 1950), 169–170.

40. Rutledge, *The Undoing of Death*, 109.

41. Paul Rowntree Clifford, *The* Reality *of the Kingdom: Making Sense of God's Reign in a World Like Ours* (Grand Rapids: Eerdmans, 1996), 83.

42. Michael Card, *Scribbling in the Sand: Christ and Creativity* (Downers Grove, IL: InterVarsity Press, 2002), 77.

43. Lewis, *Between Cross and Resurrection*, 31.

44. For a very clear and insightful summary of the biblical basis and historical development, together with the author's systematic reflections on the images of Christ as Victor, Sacrifice, and Example in the doctrine of the Atonement, see Jonathon R. Wilson, *God So Loved the World: A Christology for Disciples* (Grand Rapids: Baker Academic, 2001), 83–136. My descriptions of the gifts of each image in the sections that follow benefitted from Wilson's summaries.

45. A surprisingly balanced and spiritually thoughtful article, motivated by the controversies over Mel Gibson's movie, *The Passion of the Christ*, is Jeff Chu, et al., "Why Did Jesus Die?" *Time* 163, no. 15 (April 12, 2004): 54–61.

46. Eugene H. Peterson, "Foreword," *Get Up Off Your Knees: Preaching the U2 Catalog*, eds. Raewynne J. Whiteley and Beth Maynard (Cambridge, MA: Cowley, 2003), xiii.

47. Joel B. Greene and Mark D. Baker, *Recovering the Scandal of the Cross: Atonement in New Testament & Contemporary Contexts* (Downers Grove, IL: InterVarsity Press, 2000), 218–219 (emphasis theirs).

48. St. Athanasius, *On the Incarnation*, 37.

49. See Marva J. Dawn, *Powers, Weakness, and the Tabernacling of God* (Grand Rapids: Eerdmans, 2001) and "The Concept of 'the Principalities and Powers' in the Works of Jacques Ellul," Ph.D. diss., University of Notre Dame, 1992 (Ann Arbor, MI: University Microfilms, #9220614).

50. Douglas John Hall (following Paul Tillich) is one who discards the medieval worry about "guilt and condemnation" as not prevalent today. Tillich and Hall call "meaninglessness and despair" the primary burden of our times. See Douglas John Hall, "Despair as Pervasive Ailment," *Hope for the World*, ed. Walter Brueggemann (Louisville: Westminster John Knox, 2001), 84.

51. Leon Morris, *The Cross in the New Testament*, 2nd ed. (Grand Rapids: Eerdmans, 1999), 6.

52. Leon Morris, *The Atonement: Its Meaning and Significance* (Downers Grove, IL: InterVarsity Press, 1983), 162.

53. Evelyn Underhill, *The Ways of the Spirit*, ed. Grace Adolphsen Brame (New York: Crossroad, 2001), 68. Page references to this book in the following paragraphs are given parenthetically in the text.

54. Rutledge, *The Undoing of Death*, 63. Page references to this book in the following paragraphs are given parenthetically in the text.

55. See Fyodor Dostoevsky, *The Brothers Karamazov*, trans. Constance Garnett (New York: Barnes and Noble, 1995). I'm grateful to P. Travis Kroeker of McMaster University who pointed this out in his paper, "Dostoevsky's Apocalyptic Poetics and Monastic Spirituality: Elder Zosima on Restorative Justice," given at the American Academy of Religion/Society of Biblical Literature annual meeting in Denver on November 17, 2001.

56. The first five verses of eight, translated from a 1632 Latin office hymn by Robert Campbell (1814–1868) and sung to a Bohemian Brethren tune from 1566; #210 in the *Lutheran Book of Worship* (Minneapolis: Augsburg, 1978).

57. See Carl E. Braaten and Robert W. Jenson, *Union with Christ: The New Finnish Interpretation of Luther* (Grand Rapids: Eerdmans, 1998).

58. Clergypersons are especially singled out for venomous attacks on their supposed sanctimoniousness, but a wider reading of real-life pastors and priests and of the literature would reveal a much richer picture of greater and more genuine holiness than the caricatures display. See Raymond Chapman, compiler, *Godly and Righteous, Peevish and Perverse: Clergy and Religious in Literature and Letters: An Anthology* (Grand Rapids: Eerdmans, 2002).

59. See Stanley Hauerwas, *Sanctify Them in the Truth: Holiness Exemplified* (Nashville: Abingdon, 1998).

60. I have thought in terms of this paragraph for so long that I'm not sure if, and to whom, I might be indebted for its content. Please forgive me and enlighten me if, without noting the source, I read or heard this expression somewhere.

61. See, for example, Murray Jardine, *The Making and Unmaking of Technological Society: How Christianity Can Save Modernity From Itself* (Grand Rapids: Brazos Press, 2003) and Marva J. Dawn, *Unfettered Hope: A Call to Faithful Living in an Affluent Society* (Louisville: Westminster John Knox, 2003) and *Powers, Weakness, and the Tabernacling of God* (Grand Rapids: Eerdmans, 2001).

62. Colin E. Gunton, *The Actuality of Atonement: A Study of Metaphor, Rationality and the Christian Tradition* (Grand Rapids: Eerdmans, 1989), 158.

63. William C. Placher, *Jesus the Savior: The Meaning of Jesus Christ for Christian Faith* (Louisville: Westminster John Knox, 2001), 141.

64. See Marva J. Dawn, *How **Shall** We Worship?: Biblical Guidance for the Worship Wars*, "Vital Questions" Series (Carol Stream, IL: Tyndale House, 2003).

65. See William Schweiker and Charles Mathewes, *Having: Property and Possession in Religious and Social Life* (Grand Rapids: Eerdmans, 2004) and Dawn, *Unfettered Hope*.

66. See John Perkins, *With Justice for All* (Ventura, CA: Gospel Light, 1982) and *He's My Brother: Former Racial Foes Offer Strategies for Reconciliation* (Grand Rapids: Chosen, 1994).

67. Reported in *Chronicles of Higher Education*, March 12, 2004, and cited in "Century Marks," *Christian Century* 121, no. 7 (April 6, 2004): 7.

68. Three books which emphasize well the intertwining, besides Yoder's, which is sketched below, are P. T. Forsythe, *The Work of Christ* (Eugene, OR: Wipf and Stock, 2001 [1910]); Gunton, *The Actuality of Atonement*; and Wilson, *God So Loved the World*.

69. The most thorough answer to this is provided by N.T. Wright in his *Jesus and the Victory of God* (Minneapolis: Fortress Press, 1996), 540–611.

70. Yoder, *Preface to Theology*, 285–313, especially 288. Though Yoder offers an excellent discussion of all these themes and their strengths and weaknesses, his own alternative model does not take seriously enough our propensity to what Luther called "works righteousness." Yoder doesn't seem to appreciate deeply enough our "bondage to sin," from which we cannot free ourselves. He needs a greater emphasis on Christ working through us in the new life, rather than depending upon our own abilities to live rightly in response to His work.

71. St. Athanasius, *On the Incarnation*, 4, emphasis in the translation.

72. Everyone should read this book several times in life: Lewis, *Lion, the Witch, and the Wardrobe*, especially the death and resurrection scenes on 159–180.

73. N. T. Wright, *The Resurrection of the Son of God*, Vol. 3, *Christian Origins and the Question of God* (Minneapolis: Fortress Press, 2003), 648. Page references to this book in the following paragraphs are given parenthetically in the text.

74. Douglas Farrow, "Confessing Christ Coming," *Nicene Christianity: The Future for a New Ecumenism*, ed. Christopher R. Seitz (Grand Rapids: Brazos Press, 2003), 137.

75. Wright, *The Resurrection of the Son of God*, 655.

76. Wright, *The Resurrection*, 477, 404–405, 612, 678–679.

77. The direct referrences are in Matt. 26:62; Mark 14:62; 16:19; Luke 9:31,51; 24:51; John 1:18; 3:13; 6:62; 14:2; 20:17; Acts 1:9; 2:34; 3:21; 5:31–32.; 7:56; Rom. 8:34; 10:6; 2 Cor. 12:2; Eph. 1:20; 4:7–13; Phil. 2:9; 3:14; Col. 3:1; 1 Tim. 3:16; Heb. 1:3; 4:14; 6:19–20; 7:26; 8:4; 9:11, 24; 1 Peter 3:21–22; Rev. 11:12; 12:5.

78. Douglas Farrow, *Ascension and Ecclesia: On the Significance of the Doctrine of the Ascension for Ecclesiology and Christian Cosmology* (Grand Rapids, MI: Wm. B. Eerdmans Publishing Co., 1999), 39. Page references to this book in the following paragraphs are given parenthetically in the text.

79. Lewis, *Mere Christianity*, 167.

80. William J. Abraham, "I Believe in One Holy, Catholic, and Apostolic Church," *Nicene Christianity: The Future for a New Ecumenism*, ed. Christopher R. Seitz (Grand Rapids: Brazos Press, 2003), 180–182.

81. See, instead, Marva J. Dawn, *Joy in our Weakness: A Gift of Hope from the Book of Revelation*, rev. ed. (Grand Rapids: Eerdmans, 2002).